Grieve

Stories and Poems about Grief and Loss

Volume 4

HUNTER WRITERS CENTRE

Grieve Volume 4
Hunter Writers Centre
Newcastle NSW 2300

Email: publishing@hunterwriterscentre.org
Website: www.grieveproject.org

Grieve: Stories and Poems about Grief and Loss

22 21 20 19 18   1 2 3 4 5
ISBN-978-0-9954409-0-6 (paperback)

Cover design by HWC Publishing
Typesetting by HWC Publishing
2016 Published by Hunter Writers Centre Inc.

Table of Contents

To live is to suffer, to survive is to find some meaning in the suffering.

- Friedrich Nietzsche

Introduction

Here are stories and poems by people in the various stages of 'surviving' grief and loss. For some, 'surviving' may mean simply putting one foot in front of the other – so well described in works here that capture the raw emotion, the searing pain and the agony of simply getting through another day. For others, survival may be calmer – captured in works that show a muted sadness that comes with memories evoked by a scent or a dull, inner thud brought on by the absence of a voice.

We hope this collection of short stories and poems holds a mirror up to your situation and helps you through the words and images evoked. And, perhaps, Nietzsche may be correct in his statement if one work brings some meaning to you as you continue your journey of survival.

Karen Crofts
Director
Hunter Writers Centre
Australia
www.grieveproject.org

Calvary

Julie Watts

We dip a stick   sponge-tipped and soaked in water
into the wound of your mouth

you are thirsty
and this is our Calvary

bent knees on a white bed
your sharp bone relief

the afternoon   gathering up all its shadows.

My sister presses your hand to her cheek like a kiss
prolonged   stretching   back.

I hold your other   our skins tangled
what finger   yours   mine

fading icon   fading man
fallible as breath.

They turn you like liturgy

and we stroke the murmurless litanies of your skin
pale parchment encrypted with all our gospels

remember it ruddy and robust—throwing us high and catching
the rumbling Vesuvius of your laugh.

Driving home   kite surfers soar
above a chopped dark sea

tomorrow   I will rummage for wings
but today I curl on a stone like a plucked moth

small   flightless   shrouded in silence.

Guiding Hands

Helen Woodgate

Labour had been induced but is not progressing well. Sixteen hours. First baby. I am sweaty, exhausted, fed up. I have read all the books. Attended all the classes. I am an intelligent, educated woman birthing in a modern era. *Why is this journey so slow and stuck?*

An older midwife comes into my room. She places her hands on my belly. I look down and see wrinkled, freckly, lined hands. Her hands. They could have been my Mother's.

The memory is so intense, so unexpected.

'I want my Mum, where's Mum?' I whisper.

Raw.

I cling onto my husband, sobbing.

'Mum, I want Mum!'

The midwife and my husband exchange looks.

So much longing. So many 'gone without' moments in my thoughts. No talking into the wee hours about boyfriend troubles, no moaning about pimples or bitchy girlfriends. As a teenager I progressed into womanhood without her loving guidance. But today, I need her most of all.

But she's not here.

And she's never going to come.

Terminal cancer made sure of that.

Wave after wave of birthing pains threaten to swamp and overwhelm me. The pains mish-mash together causing chaotic contractions that do nothing except slow the birth down. I never expected this; thought I had done my grieving. It's been so long since I heard her voice. Thought I had managed to tidy up that part of my life. File closed, get on with it.

But no-one told me that I would yearn so keenly for my mother during labour. I had thought missing her on my wedding day would have been the pinnacle of loss. A girl needs her Mum on that transition day—girl to woman. Today I need her too—I am transitioning from woman to mother.

Labour and grief now attack me on all sides.

Labour strips you bare. Grief strips you bare.

I am outside of control. Rocked by pain.

I am receding into something I can't identify.

The old midwife speaks sternly to me. I ignore her at first, too exhausted to listen.

Then I am shocked by her words, her tone. She is telling me off, insisting I not be so selfish, that it is not all about me, that I am putting my baby at risk.

I should be angry but instead I smile.

My Mum would have spoken to me just . . . like . . . that.

Firm but fair.

No nonsense.

Losing myself in grief will not help me now. I have to learn to use my loss in a way I had never thought before. I must be strong, firm, just like my Mum—for my little one's sake.

'Grief and Loss' can become 'Strength and Focus'.

I will trade despair for determination. Only I can do this.

I grasp onto the midwife's hands with their wrinkles and wisdom. I get back into rhythm. It's hard and it's brutal but I must. And I never let go of those beautiful old hands until my healthy baby is born.

My Mourning

Janet Lee

They say my mourning has gone on long enough.

Those people who never came and sat beside your bed while your life slowly slipped away.

Those people who use their words as though there was some poetry in your death.

There was none.

And now there is a gaping hole where your life once sat.

They say I was lucky to have you as long as I did, those people who think grief is something which can be seen and measured, and my grieving should be less because we were together so long.

They say you were an old man and that is just the way of things. Then they walk away and talk of your death between their rounds of bowls or hands of bridge, when they pause for their tea and sandwiches.

'I called to see her but she is not doing so well,' I imagine they say, glad to have the news to tell, to play a part in my mourning.

One woman came and sang me that song from *Fiddler on the Roof*, the one which talks of sunrises and sunsets. I have no idea why.

But she meant to be kind.

Other friends came and sat, and held my hand.

They did not speak.

We had nothing to say.

I think of the nurses who cared for you. Who carried away the bloody fluid they drew from your belly. Who joked of this fluid as red wine and laughed, but were gentle with you, even as they hurt you. I suppose laughing was their way of coping with death.

I haven't found my way of coping.

Friends say stupid things: that I should look for you in the clouds, or up in the sky, that you watch over me. They say I should feel your presence.

I don't.

You are gone.

I saw the life leave your body in a slow mist.

The visits from the others are becoming less. They have paused long enough in their own busy lives. They have stopped and done the right thing, and patted and consoled and sung.

Now they leave me be.

They say I should keep the television on, the sound of the voices covering the quiet of yours.

But in truth you never spoke much.

I want to be able to grieve. To feel the emptiness. To savour the loss. To sit and mourn your passing. I want to feel the sadness of your death.

Quietly.

Alone.

I want to feel my heart breaking.

I want to cry.

I want emptiness.

I want my mourning.

Finding Grief

Jen MacCulloch

I've spent fifteen years trying to numb the hurt and push down the pain. I've tried to drown the darkness in wine and whiskey. Stuffed in food to squash and silence the sorrow. Run marathons hoping to outrun the demons.

For fifteen years I have failed.

Finally, I have given into the grief. For the past six days I have cocooned myself in my doona and cried the deepest, darkest, ugliest tears. When my mother killed herself fifteen years ago I didn't shed a single tear. It was as if the shock froze the tears. Six days ago the tears thawed and spilled out like Niagara.

These past few days I cannot recall leaving my bed cocoon and yet I know I must have sought water, food, bathroom. Today is the first day that I am conscious of being, of breathing and of needing sunlight, sustenance and cleansing.

My eyes, nose, throat and lungs ache from crying and my body is weak and waned like a wooden chair left too long in the rain. Despite these physical protests, my heart and head feel lighter and freer than they have since my mother's death. It occurs to me that all the years I'd been eschewing the pain I should have been embracing it, eyeballing it. All these years I'd been hiding had only made the grief keep on seeking. Now I was the seeker and I had found grief, called him out and won the game.

I stand under the shower which is surely my first in six days. I feel every hot droplet. I feel the suds singe my eyes. I feel my toes grip the tiles. I am aware of every hair that the pink plastic razor severs. I feel everything. It is overwhelming and a relief at once.

I wrap a scratchy towel around my middle and peer into the foggy mirror. For the first time in forever I see me and I stare at me. I smile. The first sincere, guiltless, unrehearsed smile since her death.

I have finally grieved for my mother. Let her go. Forgiven her. Released my guilt. Understood her. Known her. Laid her to rest. My days of trying to drown, stuff and outrun my grief are over. I will never spend another day that way.

I am free.

1952

Simeon Kronenberg

For my brother

1

Verdant hills, a climb of green, looked down on a yellow-lit day
      and restless, flowering garden beds, in a yard
of piled wood and purple berries for jam, where sweet-pea tendrils
      hooked to catch the sun.

2

A slight boy of five stood, one-legged on the verandah, troubled
      into trousers and the day by his grandmother.
He hopped and hung on her arm as she pulled and yanked
      at clothes suddenly too small for him. Still, he drifted,
in the garden buzz of tiger lilies and gnats.

3

Here, Mary had raised three girls alone, but Dot, her youngest suffered—
      and after two births and another long, long
despair, she was like a moth smashed onto glass.

4

She saved the sleeping pills they gave her
      and clutched them to her thin chest, like a junkie:
and in a haze of pain and grief, for the children she was leaving,
      she managed it. She left her breath
to them, nothing more.

5

And at Mary's that morning, the garden gathered around—
      and mourned with the sun—
and for the boy, the sky darkened, like a dam of black water.

Butter Chicken

James McKenzie Watson

Her arrival home is announced by the thud of her bag on the floor and the clatter of her shoes in the rack. A fleeting embrace, her jacket heavy with the cold that's followed her in. Mere minutes before we're at the dining table, eating microwaved Indian and giving the walls the thousand-yard stare. Co-inhabitants of a common exhaustion. She finally speaks through a mouthful of butter chicken.

'I don't know how you cope with all the grief in your job.'

'How so?'

'I had a client at the bank today who came straight from her daughter's funeral to cash a cheque. She said she needed to just keep doing ordinary things to keep her going but she broke down and ended up sobbing for twenty minutes. I didn't know what to do or to say. I felt so sorry for her. I just made her a cup of tea and sat with her in the end. I know this probably sounds selfish but it's so draining being around grief that's that intense. It's such a heavy, constrictive thing. It's like a big black cloud that suffocates the room.'

'Yeah. It's different when it's not your own grief.'

She looks at me with expectant eyes, waiting for my answer to the unasked question, waiting for an illumination or enlightenment to demystify the vast black cloud she speaks of. 'So how do you cope with it?'

'I guess you get desensitised after a while.'

'Come off it. I've seen the way you are when you get home sometimes. What you're like after a bad shift. You can't ever be totally desensitised, right?'

I shrug. 'Maybe not.'

'Do you grieve when a patient dies?'

'Of course I do. But if I grieved every death like it was my own family I'd have burnt out a long time ago. You can't work in a hospice and feel it that acutely.'

'It sounds kind of cold when you put it like that.'

'Well.' I stand, the two bowls to the sink, the last of the rice in the bin. 'I need to save my grief for me. The people I look after don't need another sobbing wreck at the bedside when the time comes. They need a nurse who knows what they're doing.'

I pull a jumper over my scrubs and set about lacing my work boots. She stands from the table and leans against the doorway, the fluorescent light catching her profile and highlighting her beauty.

'So what do you save your grief for?' she says. I rise towards her and she buries herself in my chest.

'For goodbyes on days like this when I only get to see you for twenty minutes before night shift. Maybe that's how I cope with grief. I try to make every second I have with you count because I've seen how much it hurts when you lose the person you love.'

She doesn't reply. The hug lingers longer than it might have otherwise.

Kathryn, Young And Dying

Linda Harding

We stood for a moment in the hall that day
and I felt 'all thumbs'
as I tried to hold onto my tumbling words.
I clunked about with awkward phrases, stumbling
into your delicate situation; a bull
in an emotional china shop.

But you,
you were fine white porcelain that day,
fragile, ephemeral, a breath away from oblivion.
So young, and so nearly gone from the earth,
you were a pastel watercolor
and all I could do was wonder
at the loveliness of you.

We spoke of the husband and child
you would leave behind, only of them,
for you had abandoned yourself,
And I remember thinking,
'How can death,
which is decay and brokenness,
be this exquisite?'
For love transformed your words to prayer,
and rays of holy beauty filled your eyes.

Your sunset proved spectacular,
it glowed behind the clouds
and seemed its brightest near the end;
hued with love and warm moments of connection.

We clutched this parting gift of your shining, tender goodbye
to our hearts, to ease the pain,
hoping that the darkness would not overwhelm us all.
It did, of course.

For you were not your beauty,
not even your love,

you were your dear self,
unique . . .
and irreplaceable.

Shattered

Sarah Bourne

My eyes are dry and sore. I haven't slept properly in over a week. When my daughter wakes, I lie next to her in the dark, listening.

'Why didn't you let me die? I want to be dead,' she repeats over and over again through her tears.

Each word is a knife in my heart.

She is twenty, her life ahead of her. I didn't see this coming, I should have. I'm her mother.

I cry with her, silently letting the tears course down my cheeks. I grieve for my daughter's happiness, for her belief in the inherent goodness in people and in life. I will hold this knowledge for her until she can take it back and set her sights on a future once more.

She is loved, but that is something else she has lost sight of. I grieve for her because she feels so alone.

Weeks pass. Some in hospital, some at home. Friends visit. She goes out with them, and I sit at home biting my thumb nail, terrified that I won't see her again, that it will be a policeman who comes to my door instead of my daughter. I text her friends to make sure she is okay. They have only gone up the road for a coffee. They are a hundred metres away. My anxiety stretches up the hill and attaches itself to her. She feels it, is angered by it, but accepts it.

My friends ask how she is. Alive, I say.

'And how are you?' they ask. I am shattered. Fragmented. I bump into bits of me that used to be part of a coherent whole; at work I get glimpses of my confidence, my competence. And then I remember. On a walk in the bush I feel a breath of happiness, until I remember.

Mostly what's left is an unrelenting fear; I teeter on the edge of panic.

I want to chain her to me. I want to make her pain go away. I want to smother her with love and make her understand that she can get through this. That we can get through this.

Because she is not alone.

On the first anniversary of her 'death day' she says she is glad she's alive.

The next year she has forgotten the date. It is of no consequence to her any longer.

But I remember. I still chew my thumb nail and watch her that little bit too closely when I know she's stressed or sad. I know there's a difference between sadness and depression, but I knew that two years ago and still missed the signs. And look what happened.

I grieve for the faith I had that I could look after my daughter and save her from pain and despair.

Codes to Leave

Linda Ireland

The late flush dahlias flare
like little disappointments.
A desultory carer smokes outside.
There are codes to enter here.

The place smells of yesterdays.
The looks are single outward journeys
shuffling each day's future tense
into something more speculative.

This is a harsh final surrendering.
In Room twenty three are your codes to leave.
You have come down to this world.
You are small now,

in this space.
Did you lift me, once,
over salty breakers at Bar Beach
where horizons rolled?

In the corridor even the light echoes.
My too loud voice is gauche.
You are moving into a silence.
All day you will stare at the wall clock.

At Steinbeck's ending
I break from my reading
and weep silently
for you my father.

You say
this is the natural order of things
and get on with the hard work
of your dying.

I am thinking of continuance
when I take your jacket to be cleaned.
They will dress you in it
at the funeral parlour.

Some weeks later
still in my handbag
five grapes in cling wrap
unravel me.

Sophia

Ted Bassingthwaighte

'I'll see you when you get back. Don't forget to get enough detail for the Coroner.'

What? I can't do this by myself. This is my first one.

'Knock on the door, introduce yourself and apply all that Academy knowledge you allegedly have.'

Constable Jones slid from behind the steering wheel of the marked police van. He slammed the door and stood staring at the dilapidated Housing Commission bungalow. There were no signs of life. The afternoon twilight and the absence of street lights made him feel uneasy. He would never admit it but in this moment he was nervous.

Knock, knock. No answer. *No-one's home. Why did they call?* he thought. He turned away. Relieved. The muffled thump of feet on wooden floor-boards echoed from inside the house. He bit his lip and waited.

A muddled-looking young woman appeared in the crack of the open door, blackness behind her.

'Yes,' she whispered.

'I'm Constable Jones. We received a call . . . .'

'I called.'

'May I come in please?'

The woman, red-faced and swollen eyed, didn't look at Jones. Pyjamas, no shoes, hair matted and disheveled. Her soft, despairing sob filled the tiny space.

The dark silent room smelt of emptiness and stale tobacco. A poverty of tired looking furniture and an ancient television the only witnesses. Apprehensive, Jones broke the uncomfortable silence.

'I want to help you. Where's your child?' he asked respectfully.

Her sobbing now a language of its own, the woman nodded towards a closed door at the far end of the room. Leaden footed, Jones neither wanted to move nor could he.

I can't do this, he thought. Still angry at his slothful Sergeant, but a sense of duty unlocked his feet. Jones approached the door with trepidation.

'Could you come with me please?' he asked.

'I . . . I can't . . . I'm sorry.'

Now a prisoner of the woman's angst, Jones took a deep breath and slowly opened the door. Fading afternoon sunlight flooded the room with a mystical haze. Soft fingers of light caressed a small timber cot standing alone in the corner. The air, musty and still. A faint odour of Johnson's Baby

Powder, reminded Jones of bath time with his own baby.

His eyes adjusted to the light and to something motionless in a pastel coloured blanket. The startling, frozen silhouette of a baby lying on its back, eyes closed and pale-faced. Jones hesitated. He reached into the cot, his trembling hand lingering a moment too long. He yearned for the baby to open its eyes. A plump tear rolled from the corner of his eye staining his shirt.

Behind him the young mother stood in the doorway twisted with grief, her eyes begging him to announce that Sophia was alive.

A Great Sadness

C.M. Sherwood

One day a Great Sadness came to visit us. I did not notice him at first.

He slid in the door quietly, grey like the fog and slow. He sat for a while in the kitchen, slumped in the corner.

My mother saw him first—well, she must have. When she hung up the phone I saw her lean on the wall, bent over, eyes closed. How could she see him with her eyes shut? She must have felt his coldness because her skin grew pale and her hands trembled.

I sat on the floor and played with the cat but I felt the coldness spread around the room. The light dimmed and I shivered, even though the sun was shining outside. I went to my room and shut the door but I could hear the Great Sadness in the kitchen, whimpering softly.

That night there was no meal on the table and I guessed he was still here and had stolen our tea. I ate some bread and dropped a long trail of breadcrumbs from the kitchen to the front door. Maybe when he was hungry again he would find his way out.

But he did not leave.

The next day a neighbour came, carrying a bowl of pasta and some muffins. I ate four muffins and no-one stopped me.

I might eat another one.

More people came to talk to my mother. They must have talked to the Great Sadness too because I saw them lean upon each other, pale and quiet, voices trembling strangely—like my mother's.

I grew angry with this intruder, stealing my food, my warmth and my mother. I had to make him go. So I laughed and shouted, broke the TV and threw my food on the floor.

But the Great Sadness stayed.

Maybe we could be friends? I crouched in the corner, silent, listening but he just grew bigger, and I watched my own skin pale and my arms and legs grow thinner. I sat in a dark, dark place for a long, long time, wondering what I should do.

One day I heard a bird singing outside the kitchen window. Its song was happy and the sun was bright. I walked out the back and sat amongst the old, dry leaves and found a pebble, shiny and grey. My skin felt warm and I could hear the wind.

I noticed the Great Sadness lurking in the shadows near the garden shed. He was much smaller than I remembered. I made him a soft bed of fallen leaves and left him my pebble.

And I realised the Great Sadness had come to live with us.

Small and quiet, he lives at the far end of our backyard.

Mostly, I forget he lives here. I go to school and ride my bike but sometimes, now and then, my mum and I take him a slice of bread.

And sit with him a while.

The Universe is Growing

Peter J. Wells

For Monica Orman

We are sucked to the dirt
By gravity, forever in a spin
As the earth itself hurtles
Round a sun, itself in motion

But we stay anchored
And without death
It is not likely we would see
The bodies leave

Flung outward
In sudden weightlessness
No wonder
Our universe expands,

Till then
We run
Out of spin and crash
Slow, like a coin

Rounding a coin funnel
Before the final wobble
Into the dark cylinder
For the Life Boats

Or the Cancer Council,
And so we dig
Our toes into the dirt
And tell stories

How we came from dirt
And will return to dirt,
Perhaps to stop the knowing
We are angels

Flung ever outward
To the outer edges
Of our universe,
A new type of gravity.

A Letter To My Dad

Ann Blackwell

Dear Dad,

Why did you do it? What the hell were you thinking? Why did you leave a good practice in Johannesburg and drag us all the way to Northern Rhodesia fifty years ago? Being made the Director of the Kitwe Hospital, did that influence you? Or was it the hunting and fishing? You must have known mum would have hated living up there. And why were you fired? None of these questions have ever been answered even though at thirteen I would have understood. The silence has gone to the graves of the people who did know, and the 'incident' lay buried in my brain for a very long time.

Do you remember that day? It was hot and I was fishing and keeping an eye out for hippos, on a rock above the Kafue River. I heard mum calling me and I tried to ignore her. I looked back, and our house seemed to be growing out of the ground like a mushroom, its earthy walls and a thick thatched roof holding it down in the middle of the African bush. Inside was cool, dark and silent. I loved sleeping under a net and watching the geckos come out at night, their little eyes shining through the thatch. The mud walls felt warm and friendly but mum's cries of, 'We live in a bloody mud hut,' kept rattling through my head.

Mum was sitting in the dining room and wanted me to try on a dress she was making. I groaned and sullenly flopped into a chair when suddenly there was an earsplitting crack that reverberated through the bush. I put my hands to my ears because they were hurting me. I looked through the window and saw you lying on the ground outside the toilet. You had blood gushing from your head and there was a rifle lying next to you.

My heart was racing. I couldn't breathe. My mind was flying everywhere. I hid under the dining room table. I closed my eyes. I thought someone had shot you. Silence hung in the still air but the insects shrieked even louder. I heard mum saying to the houseboy.

'Bring the master inside and put him on the bed.' She seemed to bring air of cool authority into the room.

'No madam,' he said, 'it is better to leave him there until the police come.'

'Oh God, is he . . . ?' Mum's voice crumbled. I opened my eyes and saw her stricken face, white with fear. She told us to get in the car, that we were going into town.

Yes, Dad we did return to South Africa, but no one would talk about the 'incident'. I just told kids at school you died of a heart attack and it lay buried in my brain. I still don't feel much except perhaps pity and every now and then a little sadness. I just cut you out of my life. Mum never spoke about you and nor did my brother. It was as though you were never there. I still don't know why you did it. No note? Perhaps you were depressed. You were certainly drinking a lot more but we just kept out of your way.

I am sorry I can't feel more tenderness towards you, but I am afraid all I feel is a huge distance between you and 'the man who used to be my father'. The feeling of silence has grown thicker over the years and now I can ask no one what happened to my father?

The Cubby House

Nikki McWatters

Your last night is going to be a sleepover. I watch as your mates build their cubby house of sheets around your bed. The ventilator churns, moving your chest up and down. You look like you are play-acting asleep to amuse the boys but we know otherwise. Your body lies there, warm and beautiful and yet, my darling, you have already flown from us. The room smells like bleach and salty tears. I wish it smelled like gardenias.

Ben and Todd are laughing as JJ struggles to tie a knot around the metal bed head. I wonder if you are watching this from somewhere far away, perhaps even close by. I let my thoughts wander back to the happier days when you were all in primary school and had chaotic sleepovers. The four of you were a force to be reckoned with and little sleep was ever had. I suspect tonight the boys will stay awake alongside you, hiding beneath the sheets with their torches, scaring themselves silly with ghost stories.

I want to lie beside you this last night and hold you like I did that first night when you were born, eighteen short years ago. One cowardly punch took you away from me and I want to make that go away, evaporate it from your timeline. I want to wrap you up in a blanket and carry you home, rubbing your skin to bring some colour back to your cheeks. Instead, tonight I will go home alone and sleep in your wooden bed with the airplane mobile hanging overhead. I will leave you and your friends to share this special last time together.

Tomorrow morning I will kiss you goodbye, a last kiss, before they take you to surgery to pay your life forward. Tomorrow is for good-bye. Tonight is for friendship.

The strength that these young men are showing as they drape sheets about the room keeps me buoyant, allowing me to smile. You are the luckiest fellow to have such wonderful buddies. They will miss you almost as much as I will if that is even possible. I will miss you with unimaginable sorrow.

The cubby house is constructed. You lie inside, shadowed and oblivious. The boys have turned this room into an exotic Arabian tent, a final adventure. Your last night will be filled with stories as the boys reminisce with you and yet without you. They are ordering pizzas. Ben laughs as he shows me his Spiderman pillow. JJ puts your teddy bear, Albert, on your pillow, nestling against your face.

These sleepovers used to drive me mad with your all-night laughter and hi-jinks. Prank calls. Truth and dare. How I wish we were still back there. I would have told you to have fun, stay up all night, eat more junk and holler at the moon.

Goodnight darling boys. Look after my baby.

Tomorrow is for good-bye, my love. Tonight it is cubby house time.

What Would You Say?

Gregory Klemm

Driving to the beach the other day, you were in the car beside me and it made me happy. I was talking to you and you were smiling. I made up things that you would say and we laughed together. Without even turning to look at you, I could see you. I could feel your aura, your beautiful glow which permeated the car, filling me. It worried me when I realised what I was doing. But I didn't stop. I talked with you all the way to the coast. Though sometimes we sat in silence, too, not needing to say anything. Just contented.

When I arrived I had tears streaming down my face. I sat in the car crying. I didn't want to leave you. I wanted to stay in the car and just keep on talking to you. You couldn't come with me. People would look at me strangely. They would worry about me. Well meaning people, of course. They just wouldn't understand.

It's been more than six months now. I hardly sleep. I go to work in a fog, and somehow muddle through the day. I don't know how I keep going.

Every night I lie awake and talk with you. I pull you to me and I can feel you, I swear I can feel you pressed against me. And we talk about my day, and your day, and our friends, and we laugh. But sooner or later we always come back to that same topic. I don't want us to fight, but I can't help myself from asking. Why did you leave me? Why did you leave me here alone?

And the problem is that even though I know almost everything you would say, and I could talk to you for eternity filling in your words for you, I don't know what you would say about that. And I don't know what you would tell me to do. And nothing that I imagine you saying sounds right so we always end up fighting. And eventually dawn comes, and the pain and anxiety of the dark turns to a dull, throbbing ache as light slowly seeps in. Somehow I find the strength to pull myself from bed to start the day's routine.

I love you. I miss you so much. I would give anything for you to be here with me now, because I know I could get through this if only I could just talk to you about it. I know I could find the strength to let you go, if only I could have you here to help me do it.

Pippa

Janeen Samuel

One by one
we are picking up and tidying away
the things you left behind—
bowls from the verandah;
cushion from the office floor;
old crumpled blanket from the corner of the kitchen;
frayed length of rope and half-chewed tennis balls;
most of all—
all over the garden and orchard—
bones. Who would have thought
one small dog could leave
so many belongings?

One by one
we are giving up and tidying away
all the old habits—
bracing oneself for the early morning greeting;
warmth of a weight in the lap;
a hand let down from the chair for a tongue's caressing;
most of all—
all over the garden and orchard—
the eager feet beside us. Who would have thought
one small spirit could leave
so many empty spaces?

Dragonflies And Other Visitations

Anne Elvey

Dragonflies hover in the nursing home carpark.
Our two lives flow from the hour when an eyelash

swam in an eye. Insects have abandoned your lamp.
They halo your wits' hum. Grey dissolves

into the spectrum of dawn. Two split pomegranates
bleached pink and dun grasp a bare limb.

On my side-mirror a carapace is fixed in a web.
You tug at your mask. In its last season your tree

either refuses to bloom, or is profligate with blossom.
Doctors speak of fluid around your heart. Their pump

is nearly too loud to hear the answer they ask.
A coarse thread unwinds from the aureole of my breast

and makes a gash in the road. Neon and steel
abrade the kerb. Our refuse has gone. What's left

is thud. I bring in the bins, carry your dream
in my work and ask if it dies with you. A raven

perches on your chair. Ivy is reaching to entwine
the spokes. Wheels glint with vernal sun.

The air has warmed. Your late aspiration nests.
I am waiting for the wind to blow pollen

across my page. Under a bird-net an insect whirrs
then stops. The long abdomen curves from its thorax

beneath a round head. The facets of its globes
and the outstretched wings are quick and still.

I lift the net. A yellow emperor flies off.
Morning, I wake to the line: the dead

give us royalties, the hard way. A mosquito net
of translucent wings falls over my road.

A Lifetime In An Hour

Angela Ticehurst

'You will have an hour with her,' they told me as I clutched the phone. Only one hour.

That doesn't seem like a lot of time I thought to myself, but outwardly I replied, 'Ok, thank you for organising everything for me.'

I hung up the phone and looked at my husband.

'We have an hour on Wednesday, the day before the funeral' I told him. I could tell by the look in his eyes he still wasn't sure about any of this, but I knew when push came to shove, he would be standing by my side as always.

Wednesday arrived. As we drove there we didn't speak, both scared and nervous of the hour ahead of us. I had given birth to my stillborn daughter six days earlier, and now I would finally get to be with her. My only memory of my baby was pain, deafening silence, and a broken heart. It was time to add another memory.

There was so much I wanted to say, so many thoughts racing through my head. How do you fit a lifetime of love and plans into one hour?

As I walked in I could barely breathe, the pain almost overwhelming. When my daughter was put in my arms my vision blurred as the tears fell. She was so beautiful. I couldn't take my eyes off my angel. She was perfect. I just kept touching her face, her nose, her cheeks. Her skin was so cold and it made my heart break more.

As I looked at my baby, I wanted to tell her how much I loved her. I wanted her to know that I had never loved anyone more than I did her, that she taught me what true love really was. I wanted to tell her I was sorry. I had one job in this world, and that was to protect her and keep her safe, and I had failed. I wanted to apologise for my body failing her, for failing her as a mother and how I wished more than anything that

I could've changed places with her. But all I could do was stare at her and touch her face, I just couldn't find the words.

I wanted to freeze time and stay in that room forever. I wanted her to open her eyes and look at me. I wanted to see her first smile, hear her first laugh, have her grip my finger with her tiny little hand. I wanted to send her to her first day of school and one day talk about boys. I wanted to watch her grow and see the woman she would become. There's a whole lifetime worth of memories that were taken away from me, so many firsts that I never got to experience. I only had that one hour.

When I handed my daughter back, a piece of my heart went with her. As I walked away with empty arms . . . again.

Skin To Skin. Breath To Air.

P. J. Turnbull

Pulling out each pulsating vein. One by one. They were heavily weighted with her own possibility, but she finally felt weightless as she knitted them into a jumper to keep him warm. She'd never felt so big and so small as when she was holding his tiny head in her hands. Every little atom of him had depended on her and now her only consolation was that their atoms were once both stardust, though she doubts the stars they came from were part of the same constellation or even cosmos. He felt so far away even though he was so close. Skin to skin. Breath to air.

It was hard to believe that this child was of her own flesh and blood. He seemed too alien, too foreign. When she was carrying him her stomach swelled, little lines appeared writing the story of him all over her body. At one stage she felt her skin become red and itchy as if it was trying to reject something. An unfamiliar object? A disease? No, something much worse: his life. She carried him within her, a literal dead weight constantly pulling her back down as she tried to float towards a cloud of hopeful delusion. When he left she felt the blunt sting of loss in the now hollow cavern at the depth of her core. The stinging didn't cease; it grew and he didn't. The word unfair will always fall short as it strains to reach out and grant him true justice. The feat it must have been to stop his small frame from crushing under all of the dread. But here he is. Skin to skin. Breath to air.

His little body remained still, and as she held him everything around her slowed. It was him and her, nothing existed before and she dared not to think about after. She had created life, even if all his life knew was death. He still existed. For her that was enough because it had to be. Skin to skin. Breath to air.

Neatly packaging this excruciating feeling into beautiful and easy to digest words is impossible. Grief has sharp and jagged edges that catch on your throat as you try to swallow it and let it pass through you. But it doesn't pass through you; it stays with you, it travels with you, it lives with you. It's there when you see everyone else deliver their beautiful bundles of joy. Grief eclipsed joy; you received apologies instead of congratulations, knowing looks instead of smiles. It's still there. It's there and it doesn't make sense. Like a sentence spoken in a foreign language that you just cannot grasp, it's too fast and you're too slow, and the quiet burn of confusion continues long after the final word is said. Your bundle was not one of joy, but it was yours. He will always be yours. Skin to skin. Breath to air.

How Many Patients Can I See In One House Call?

Hilton Koppe

I am just an ordinary man. Such an ordinary man. Yet sometimes I am asked to do the most extraordinary things.

I've been dreading this moment. For weeks. I knew it was coming. Ever since Greta invited me to be her family doctor, I knew all roads led to this point.

Greta has ovarian cancer. Like my mum had, before she died. Greta has had surgery and chemotherapy. Like my mum had. Greta's treatment held her cancer at bay for a time. Like my mum's had. Greta's cancer came back. Like my mum's had.

And now this moment. The first home visit. The moment which heralds the beginning of the end. As I drive to Greta's home, my mum is in the car with me, seated by my side. Encouraging me, as always. Reminding me to focus on Greta. Not the past.

I am met at the front door by Alice. Alice is a Home Care worker. She is also a patient of mine. There, floating above Alice, is her husband Dave. He had been a patient of mine too. Before he died from oesophageal cancer. About eighteen months earlier.

Floating just behind Dave is John. John was a friend of mine from our soccer team. And a patient. He died from bowel cancer. A year after his only child was born. Both Dave and John give me an encouraging smile and vanish as I enter Greta's home.

Alice calls out to Greta and her partner, 'The doctor's here.' I am transported back to Ted's home. Ted was dying from leukaemia. It was my first home visit. The house was filled with the noise of his children and grand-children. But things became hushed with the announcement of the doctor's arrival.

Greta is in bed. I examine her distended belly. I can feel the tumours regrowing. And I am thrown back with my mum. In her doctor's room. As he examined her distended belly and said that he could feel her tumours regrowing.

Greta's partner accompanies me to the front door, asking me the questions so common at this stage of a serious illness. 'How much longer does she have? What will happen from here? What more can I do?' I answer the questions as best as I can. As I had for Katie's parents and Smithy's wife and Thelma's husband and Kevin's children.

I retreat through the crowds to the sanctity of my car. I am surprised to see Macca in the back seat.

'You never fucking came to visit me,' he sneers. Macca was one of my more colourful patients.

'I did visit you,' I retort. But it was after he had unexpectedly died. To sign his death certificate.

Suddenly, they are gone. All of them. Gone. Leaving me alone. Completely alone.

An ordinary man. Such an ordinary man. Who sometimes is asked to do the most extraordinary things.

Shooting Ducks

Jessie Ansons

'Roll up, roll up!'

Stan pushes me gently toward the shooting duck game. We're at the carnival.

Not the best place to make a decision like this.

But where is a good place?

I haven't said a word to Stan since we left the doctor's office. She's given us twenty-four hours to think about it. The options are clear, the decision is not.

Stan's bought me a stick of fairy-floss. I hold onto it tightly in my left hand, untouched. When Stan first handed it to me I'd stared at it for a full minute.

He's trying to stay upbeat. Trying to take my mind off it.

The joyous screams of children on a nearby rollercoaster drift by.

The doctor said there's a one-in-ten chance that something's wrong with the baby.

Our baby.

I look up at the row of metal ducks moving quickly before my eyes. Yellow, yellow, yellow, red. The loaded gun is on the table in front of me.

'Try to shoot the red duck!'

I think back to the day we found out we were pregnant. We'd cuddled together on the lounge and talked about our dreams of the future: the nursery, our baby's first steps, trips to the carnival.

Fairy-floss.

The worker at the shooting duck game has mustard in his beard.

'Pick up the gun and try for a red duck! A one-in-ten chance!'

All this time, we've kept the pregnancy our little secret, waiting for the right moment to share the news with friends and family. What news would we now be sharing? Would we share the news at all?

In the car on the way to the carnival Stan's voice croaked into the silence. He said that it was my decision. That he would support me in whatever I chose to do.

And that didn't help at all.

It's as if there's ten ducks in my belly. Nine perfect fluffy yellow ducks that would make Stan the happiest man alive. But in the mix there's the hardened metal duck.

The red duck.

The screams of the rollercoaster drift by once more. Stan glances at the ducks, then asks, 'Would you like a turn?'

It's dark, but the neon lights around us have made Stan's face turn green. He doesn't look well.

No one has died. but we are already grieving. We're grieving our lost dream. The dream where we come to the carnival, a toddler between us swinging from our hands. The dream where we release our laughter into the night sky and we're oblivious to any wrong in this world.

My eyes follow the ducks. They move faster and faster until they're nothing but a blur. A smudge of yellow with a flash of red.

Am I allowed to grieve for one I kill?

I let the fairy-floss fall to the ground. And pick up the gun.

For That Way Madness Lies

Valerie Volk

Mourning can make madmen of us all.
I feel impelled to do things out of character—
strange, even idiotic, acts.
I think to have good friends to dinner,
place in an empty chair your photograph,
so that you're here, with us once more.
I shake my head in wonder as I see
normality break down, and recognise a fear—
deep-seated—that grief can turn wits lunatic.

It's like that moment when they wheeled you from the room:
the nurses looking solemn, family in tears,
and, suitably restrained, the kindly men
who covered you in velvet pall before they took you
for their distant ministrations.
I watched dry-eyed, wondering what they'd do
if all those years of deep-embedded fortitude,
the socialised constraints, propriety, broke down
as dam walls shattered and anguish flooded out.
I suddenly could understand the sisterhood of mourners
who fling themselves upon the funeral pyre
or, screaming, tear their hair in chunks and rend their clothes.
I could have followed wailing down that corridor
and hurled my misery upon your still-warm form,
in desperate effort to prevent you going.

But no, we have been trained to show endurance
and smile, no matter how we suffer.
So there will be no dinner parties with you there,
a captured image of your former self.
Although it would be interesting to see
how others would embrace a situation
so far beyond all expectation of a woman
who has always shown a proper public face.

Hovering

Nikki McWatters

You are not dead. That is the sliver of hope I cling to. And yet I mourn the loss of your innocence, your dignity and your power.

I cannot say the word without tasting bile but I will not shy from it. I will not let it have that power over me. *Heroin*. I hate it with every fibre and sinew in my body. It is a demon of such devastating possession; a liar, a thief and a serial killer. It has its bony fingers around your throat, its other hand gripping your pulsing heart. It is a jealous lover, a coward puncher, a blood-stained dagger.

You are not dead. That is all that lets me catch brief snippets of sleep between squally black nightmares. And yet I grieve for the little boy with the sunshine smile and the diamante blue laughing-eyes.

Heroin. It takes your money and it shreds your soul. Every time the phone rings I die a little, crumble at the edges and thread my cross-wires a little tighter. Every time you ask me for money I shadow box my excuses, arguing that you'll get it anyway, with or without my cash. I give you too much hoping it might buy you better quality, staving off the almost inevitable. And then I wonder if I've done the right thing. Or not. Next time I cry poor and hope you don't have to do anything too terrible to scramble for a fix. Maybe you'll go without. I know you won't.

You are not dead. That keeps me reaching forward to a pipe-dreamed future where you have slain the dragon and walk tall with clear eyes and the curl of a grin. Anything but the hollow-cheeked, pin-pricked gaze of the zombie that looks back at me when you visit.

Heroin. It assaults your body, ravages your spirit and drowns your artistic ambitions. Hiding in the alley-ways, burning on a spoon, gnawing away at your life like a street-dog on a bone, it cannot stand light. It cannot abide love. It speaks a language of desperation and abomination. I want to take it and wrestle it from your life and sever its head, but I know that only you can do that. All I can do is keep loving you. I offer you help, rehab, my hugs. You don't want any of that. You only want one thing. Only that one thing.

You are not dead. But while you dance with the devil, death hovers over you like an invisible buzzard. I want my love to keep you safe. I want my baby home, tucked into bed with a warm cup of milk. You are not dead. And every day I cry wracking sobs of thanks for that fragile mercy.

I love you.

Mum.

The Death Of Small Things

Elizabeth Egan

First, the foetus.
She is aglow mid-term when he slips away.
The gasping mewl is a death rattle—cardboard lungs do not transfer
oxygen.

Corrosive guilt wells like frothing soda.
Grief lodges wherever blood flows.

Hopeful of a butterfly she places
a cocoon of twigs and silk in a box.
Time reveals . . . nothing.
It was sucked to desiccation
by a wasp to feed its young.
Her bones are heavy:
she failed to nurture an insect.

One mouse of a plague drops into a sudsy sink—paddles frantically:
she pins it under a potato-masher.
The pulsing fight throbs up her arm
for longer than the echo of that dolorous cry.
Her babe had not such strength.
The sodden corpse is fished out with a serving spoon:
she is a murderer.

Birds strike the car head on,
fat lizards bask where wheels must go,
in the cat's mouth, a fairy wren, saliva wet, unscarred.

Death, emboldened, is attendant.
The Furies ride with her, harvesting innocents—a role reversed.

Keep away, keep away, she warns Small Things:
my thoughts wound, my touch kills.
Such odd notions enchant and terrify.

Haunted by the hideous gift she is suspicious in recovery:
bans insect sprays, carries spiders outside,
decrees her next pet will be a rescue dog.

Spring. The chance of redemption—she is with child again.

Exotic

Linda Ireland

Perfect in Dublin's Botanical Gardens
the tulip beauties celebrate themselves.
Like teasing girls they stare and sway.
I turn my reluctant back on them
to walk for ages amongst plants of
every wonderful shape and shade.

But here is the true exotic of the day
growing wild in the hothouse of the café.
Among the doughy conversations,
shots of coffee grain laughter
and tea cups whispering steam,
a young boy alone at a table moaning,

rocking on the short stalk of his body,
swivelling his head from side to side,
his blind and shocking eyes
cobalt flowers without stamens.
Propped cross legged on a chair,
he drools and croons, a hybrid.

We around him fresh from our garden walks
politely dig at dainty morning treats
with little silver forks
and swallow pity and relief
in equal parts, unsettled,
eyes anywhere but there.

Mother and father return with cafe trays.
Root stocked to their voices
his rocking moaning works a pitch that pierces
every corner of a room now stilled.
                    Dadda!
He shouts his solitary word, exalts it.

Tenderly the father feeds his son, scooping food
into a mouth no girl will want to kiss.
The mother smiles and leans across
to wipe a crumb from her husband's cheek.
They flare like the tulips,
suddenly lovelier.

The Toothbrush Incident

Angela J. Maher

Elizabeth froze in the bathroom doorway, her eyes riveted to the toothbrush holder. Pale pink, ceramic and decorated in poorly painted flowers, it held no threat. It sat in its usual spot on the right-hand side of the sink. Such an ordinary object but, at that moment, it held all the pain in her world.

Two toothbrushes were in its embrace; one red, one blue. They leant towards each other, lovers about to kiss. The bristles of the blue toothbrush were in disarray. The bird's nest of fibres, now ineffectual in their job, hinted at imminent replacement. A replacement that would never happen.

Elizabeth slumped to the floor, contorted face hidden behind cold, trembling hands. Everywhere held a reminder that life would never be the same. The simplest of objects could become a thorn that pricked at her soul, bringing forth tears that surely should have dried up by now.

She remembered a face, leaning close to hers in the moment before a kiss. Hazel eyes drifting closed, a perfect nose she had imagined on her future children, lips whose touch she could still feel. The vision was replaced in an instant by another one of the same face. Unwelcome, a recurring memory appeared of his face pale and motionless. He looked like he was sleeping, but the eyes stubbornly refused to flicker open.

Separation for more than even just a few hours had not been the plan. An unsigned marriage certificate had not been the plan. A house of hollow echoes had not been the plan. The plan had been marriage, and children, a vegetable garden, bright yellow roses framing a Federation style house. The future was no longer a plan, and it cut to her core.

Gathering the frayed strings of her remaining strength, Elizabeth stood. Keeping her eyes averted from the toothbrush holder, she moved across and groped blindly for the cheap plastic reminder of what would never be. Her fingers closed around both, and she flung them into the bin at her feet. A hesitation and the holder itself followed them, the hollow clunk of fracturing ceramic mirroring her heart.

Argyle Socks

Audrey M. Molloy

She cries herself awake.
Tears cross her temple, prickle her scalp.
The surgeon holding her hand
stays longer than she expects.
The anaesthetist too was kind
until his faux pas: *How many weeks?*
(You mean, since it died?)
Her cheek burns; curved mirrors,
brash lights—illuminating her
like a fossil dig at night.

A text message: *On my way*
In he strides—shiny-shoed, stripy-tied,
phone clamped to his ear—
rolls his eyes, spirals his finger in the air
in a 'wrap it up' sort of way.

She is on intimate terms with the drill:
The people he is dealing with are *clowns*
The deal he is working on is *a circus*
Now he sits on the chair, one brogued foot
across the other knee,
raps out his strange language
like an auctioneer at a cattle mart
grey-market   seventy-off   value-prop.

The blue gown's ties chafe her neck.
She dresses gingerly: knickers   jeans
bra   sweater   socks   boots   coat.
A pen stabs the form; she can go.
They walk in the same direction;
doors *shoosh* open to the speckled air.

The chirp of the car unlocking,
the growl of the engine   the squeak of the wipers
the patter of his words on the phone
all the way home.
Years later, she recalls most clearly
the diamond pattern of his socks.

Pretty Lies A Lost Heart

Abigail Cini

There is a tiny flap of yellow in the corner of my locker. I scroll through my combination, remove the lock and the sticky note slides down. Unfolding the tiny piece of paper reveals hasty, scribbled writing.

Nobody likes you.

The words come like heartbeats: short, consistent and visceral like blood. In that delicate moment when collapsing is far too easy, everything is still. Every breath, every word, every sound channels through me but I don't react. Is anyone watching? Are they waiting for my reaction? Are they watching the wave break over me and throw me onto the beach? Like so many tiny pebbles, I skitter wildly up the shore in its wake. I just know that I can't be here, so I run. I just want to have the time back. Back to when you could trust a smile.

The sadness is real now. It pierces into my arteries and slows my blood down like lead. My eyelids flutter, pushing away tears that burn. Bec was my best friend. A best friend can bring you back to life when you are in a really dark place but what do you do when your best friend is the person who pushed you there? She was the one friend I thought I would never lose; the one I thought would last my whole life. Now things are different and awkward. I want to talk, but all I get is her voicemail. We didn't have a fight. There were no pointed fingers, no apologies asked for. There was simply an absence of friendship overnight. It's really hard not talking to the person to whom you used to talk to every day. The silence between builds an awful wreckage, one held up by pillars of loneliness and unworthiness.

People who leave you behind leave something even more painful than goodbyes. It is the absence of a goodbye that cuts. You cannot help but wonder which aspect of your personality was so dreadful. You suddenly become so vulnerable to the world like an origami heart that is pulled down into the sea and melts into nothingness.

I buy my lunch from the cafeteria now because it gives me time to scan the yard for an empty space. I stop when I see Bec. Her hair is different; she has bangs and blonde highlights. I can be overlooked, I can be replaced. It makes me feel as substantial and alive as a pressed flower. I can't shake the feeling that I am the topic for today's Session. They all know what to say, like some code that is built into their bones.

This friendship is broken and so is a piece of my heart.

The Cow Jumped Over The Moon

Dominique Hecq

I have not looked outside
since I papered the house
sealed all doors and windows

I have not seen the light
thin to dark at sunset
the clouds that move fast
in the sky the moon dusting
the buds that grow leaves

I have not seen the mould
on the pomegranates

I have not hummed the roses
dead on their smelly stems

I have eaten nothing
and nothing has eaten
all the words in my mouth

I have not heard my son
whose voice had just broken

I have not touched his room

The Last Dressing

Margaret Jackson

'Victoria, you haven't looked at your wound yet, have you?' says the visiting nurse as she smooths the dressing onto my skin. She's been calling to change the dressings since I came home from the hospital. I turn my face back to her.

'No. I'll get to it soon.'

'Well you need to. I know it can be frightening but you need to get acquainted with the change in your body. This is my last visit and this is the last dressing. You'll have to take it off yourself.'

I draw back from the pity in her eyes; from the judgment I imagine I see there.

She packs away her paraphernalia as easily as she expects me to pack away my loss; as easily as the doctors cut off my breast.

I want to scream at her: 'You don't understand what this means.'

This was the breast my babies nursed at. It was part of who I rejoiced in becoming—a mother. This was the breast Brooke dampened with her tears as she sobbed her heart out over that first horrid boyfriend who dumped her for someone easier. I feel again the crush of Shaun's young body against my breast as he hugged me in the delight of winning his first swimming trophy.

Now there is this gap, this mutilation that I can't look at. And if I can't bear to look at it, how can Michael? My husband Michael loved our intimate moments as we clasped skin to skin. Will he turn away in disgust?

I shake myself out of my thoughts and show the nurse out. I close the door firmly and stalk to the hall mirror. I look into my own dull eyes. The nurse is right. I have to look. I have to accept. It's part of who I am now.

Oh God. I screw my eyes shut then take a deep breath.

I'll get up early tomorrow before Michael wakes.

I'll go into the shower where the water can conceal the tears.

I'll peel back the last dressing and see my mutilated body.

I turn the water to warm. I drop my night shirt and step into the flow. Carefully and slowly I peel off the dressing and look down. A high wailing sound escapes from deep in my throat, and echoes in the bathroom. I turn to the wall and lean my hands against it to hold myself up.

Strong hands grasp my shoulders and turn me. Gently I am enclosed in Michael's arms and held, skin to skin against his chest. Together we stand while the water flows over us.

Letter, Unsent

Ronald Pretty

I have tried. Night after night
I sit here, a pen in my hand
& whisky beside me in a futile search
for words. Not any words, but those

that can tell without cant,
without flourish, of my sadness,
the sorrow I feel at what
has been visited upon you;

& even now as I try to write, again
I can hear your ironic voice: I hope
it makes you feel better, sport,
because it does nothing for me.

Swallow your tears, I hear you say,
it's not pity I want, but shiraz or pot
or prescription painkillers to give me
the strength to wake each morning,

to face the day without counting,
to walk the dogs & feel the sun on my face,
to taste without fear what this day has
to offer. Talk to me if you can provide

such pleasure, such peace. When I visit,
you smile, you sometimes laugh.
Your mind, your tongue has lost none
of its edge, none of its wit or sardonic humour.

Once home, I try again; I want
& do not want to write to you,
for I never can find the words.
So much is gush, irrelevant & useless.

Sitting here bleeding ink again tonight,
I know this is another letter I will not send.
Sleep well, old friend: I'll never find the words,
but my love, my care is with you always.

Ironbark

Chloë Callistemon

they carry him down the aisle, their shoulders
quake under the weight of the ironbark coffin, a hand slips
his daughter sings and the morning ruptures

glassed colour stains her face, drips
blue and red onto white flowers, onto bodies left to
quake under the weight of the ironbark coffin, a hand slips

into another hand, others grip air, cloth, flower, pew
I pick at the scab on my knee, blink
blue and red onto white flowers, onto bodies left to

shrink with her voice as she begins to sink
under the last long note, finished as it broke her throat
I pick at the scab on my knee, blink

away the bleak faces at the back, staring, remote
look up at the strange windows until the glass blurs
under the last long note, finished as it broke her throat

wet breaths chafe the quiet, the crowd stirs
they carry him down the aisle, their shoulders
almost steady, eyes fixed, they turn their back on hers
his daughter sings and the morning ruptures

My Father, Swimming

Helen Bradwell

I always stand a long time with the sea
around my knees—tasting the cold,
adjusting to its bite before I dive.

You leapt straight in. You moved in water like
a secret acrobat, so easy with
the rough and tumble of the waves, looping
and rolling, free of breath and flesh,
moulding the sea to form strong certain shapes,
my children yelling as you'd snatch them up
to hurl them squealing, laughing in the waves.

The sea's still drawing up along the sand.
It's hard to know there'll never be a chance
to watch you surface with that gannet grace,
the water running off you silver, gray.

I have to trust you're swimming headlong still
and waiting for us just around the bay.

Daughter Of Grief

Diana Threlfo

I hold my breath and listen at the door of my mother's bedroom. Is she awake, asleep . . . alive? The door groans when I nudge it ajar. I blink into the darkness, make out her face among the pillows and tiptoe into the room. My mother stirs and I breathe out.

Yesterday, a shaft of sunlight beamed through a chink in the curtains. Now the curtains are drawn more tightly than ever.

'Okay if I turn on the lamp?' I ask sitting down on the edge of the bed.

I don't wait for her reply and the dim light glows through the red lampshade. My mother turns her head and gazes at me. Her enlarged pupils deaden her brown eyes. Her olive skin looks sallow and sags against her cheekbones. When I smooth her hair my hand recoils at its brittleness. The smell of stale perfume, mustiness and dust fills the room.

What demons drove her in here this time? Are they the same tormentors or new creations of her mind? Or . . . was it something I did?

'Can I get you anything?' I ask.

She reaches for the bedside table. Fumbles around. When she finds a foil medication strip she breaks out two capsules and pushes them into her mouth. I pour the last of the water from a jug into a tumbler and hand it to her. She takes a swig and swallows the capsules.

'Could you refill the jug?'

Her speech is thick and slurred, as though her tongue's too large. I stand, pick up the empty jug and look down at her figure huddled beneath the bedclothes.

What comfort does she hope to find in this gloom? What cure for the melancholy that fifteen dragging days have failed to deliver?

In the kitchen it takes mere moments to fill the jug. But in those moments memories crowd my mind. Laughter. Spontaneous. Effortless. My mother's laughter at her Jack Russel's antics, at jokes told by dinner guests and at an old television clip of Lucille Ball trampling wine grapes. I remember my mother's arm linked through mine as we strolled along the beach-front, her ready smile shining warmly in her eyes, and when I recall her hugs I can almost feel her arms enfold me, smell the spiced fragrance of her favourite perfume.

Has she forgotten? Forgotten it all? Surely she remembers she has a daughter?

A shudder interrupts my thoughts. I stare at the jug. Then I lift it from the draining board and head back to the bedroom. The drugs have taken affect; my mother snores lightly. But even in sleep her brow is furrowed and her lips are tightly stretched. I half fill her tumbler with fresh water and put the jug back on the table. Then I straighten the covers across her sleeping form, kiss her forehead and switch off the lamp.

Before I leave I tug open the curtains, just enough to let in some light.

For Michael

R. H. Butler

I still remember the specialist's waiting room, how we flicked through magazines as though we were merely there waiting to see the doctor about a common cold. We'd been in this surgery so many times before, seen this doctor for years.

I knew before he said it. Even before he'd ushered us into his room, closed the door and sat us down in those grey armchairs with a tissue box on a small short table in front of us.

There was nothing left to try. Nothing they could do. Terminal.

But I didn't want to lose you.

I found the 'miracle man' on the internet, the neurosurgeon who operated on the inoperable, who could cure the incurable.

He was realistic: there was only a thirty percent chance of success, and even then it would only be a reprisal, not a cure—not for your type of cancer. But I knew you would be one of those thirty in one hundred. And every moment is precious. Even if it's a couple more days. Right?

If we had foreseen it, would we have chosen differently? Would I have been so adamant we try? The complications. The meningitis you contracted as a result of the operation that meant you had to stay in hospital for months. The meningitis that meant you couldn't take the drugs that would stop the tumour from growing back. And it did. Grow back. Before you left hospital, it was the same size it had been before the operation.

But we celebrated when you came home. We ate pizza. I lit candles, and you stood long enough so we could rock from side to side in each other's arms, listening to Sade.

It was after we danced you told me.

I didn't want to hear it. I wanted you to hang on. To hope. To fight. I wanted you to believe my obvious delusion: if you kept fighting you would win. But you'd already fought for yourself, for your family and friends, and for me. You had given us more time. Now time, for you, was pain and you wanted it to end.

And in the parts of me I didn't want to heed, I wanted what you wanted.

But how could I want you to die?

It's strange how once our tears of anger, of bitterness, of hopelessness were shed, you and I reconciled our grief. The hardest decision had been made. Now it was done you could go back to living, you said.

It was only another two months. Sixty one days and seven hours. Days that felt long and forever and, yet, looking back, seemed as short as a few moments.

And then you were gone, a breath of breeze moving the curtains after the last faint rise and fall of your chest; our cat curled at the foot of the bed, opening her eyes and looking at the window.

She sits by that window often. So do I. Waiting for the breeze.

Go Gentle

Sascha Morrell

Vision dims as the day dies and the rocky slope runs crumbling into the sea. It's barely winter, but already the wind has turned on us. We stand shoulder to shoulder in its salt sting. You stood taller than me once but now you hunch, a bony ghost. Your face is creased with lost years.

I wonder how many times we have stood here facing the horizon, tracing the line where the sea meets the sky. From this spot, we used to think we could make out the curve of the world. Now I imagine how it will roll on without you, and how I will have to go on with everything eroding, blowing cold, falling away.

Even when the winds are big, the gulls hold onto the headland. More of them every year. They huddle on the grass, dotting the slope where the hard air ruffles their feathers. They seem to mourn with me, rending the air with white cries.

I take your hand. Come on now. I lead you inside like a child, leaving behind what is left of the view.

I microwave two frozen meals, put out two placemats, the water jug, cups and cutlery, your medication. I fasten the big napkin around your neck. You watch me with a wary, watery gaze that turns me into a stranger. I'm getting used to it now, this look, where your eyes seem to grieve for all they have seen and forgotten, straining and searching my face for something they no longer recognise.

There is none of your mumbling tonight, no moaning protest. But you are slow. You struggle with the cutlery, years knotting in your knuckles. As usual I chat away, though tonight you don't listen. I talk about the time you saw Halley's Comet, your Morris Minor, the time your dad shook hands with Neil Armstrong.

I try to remember your memories. Every day I tell them to you like stories and sometimes, just for a moment, you seem to resurface, rising to meet me. I get a glimpse of you, urgent and fleeting, then it fades. Not tonight.

On the table before us is a vase of everlastings.

I treasure the terrible time we have left. I treasure the giddying tilt of your decline.

After the late news, leaving you adrift in your recliner, I step outside for some fresh air. The wind has died down slightly and I wander out a little from the house, barefoot in the wet grass. The sky is a dull, heavy gloom. It is as if the sea's boom and roar has no source, and there is neither headland nor horizon, no edges and no end.

I move forward by blind instinct, with a careful, uncertain tread. My presence unsettles the gulls. Then the breeze picks up in a sudden gust and two of the birds lift their wings, then four or five, revealing their whiteness in flight. In the dark they might be doves, except they're screaming.

The Wardrobe

Avril Bradley

How many years, two, three?
And finally, I have the fortitude
to dismantle the margins,
the tangible accoutrements of your life,
expressions of our shared scenes, treasures
I keep to have something of you, still with me.

Your clothes are still
where you left them.

I open the wardrobe door.
You emerge in a grey waisted dress
a favourite until you were too wasted
to wear it. But now here you are smiling.
I take the hand you offer.
Kiss its sunburnt edge
before the flesh melts from bone
and you are gone.

In a dark recess, a heap of summer nothings
forget themselves, as you did in the end.
Crumpled now, I hold the bikini you wore
when we found that first beauty spot.
Then, I kissed its dark speculation.

Now, I tremble at the afterthought
of your sleep in the hot noonday sun.

The empty bag is heavy in my hand.
I steady by the wardrobe's rail.
Pluck the dark business suit
made shiny from the wear of work.
It slides easily from the hanger
no longer endowed with your will.
The last dust of determination falls on the floor.

Once More In Goroka

Allan Padgett

You lay there, waiting patiently.
We gathered in good grace to say goodbye—
and to thank you for your being. It was a restless,
tear-drenched six days later—clearly by now
you had become the post-you.
The long white van pulled
up, you slipped inside
and the driver took you away,
along that busy broad promenade
of faded dreaming, took you
to the vapourising place
toward the sea. I swear a cloud
of birdwings, sapphire and flashing
scythes of smitten light,
hovered over you—
watching, waiting, guarding.
On a later day you arrived
in Port Moresby, where you await
your final journey:
to be tipped and then to flutter
free as dusty motes
above your beloved, rainfed Goroka
and then be washed to settle soilward,
where your essence will remain—
as your memories recirculate
to fertilise imagination, excite a jabber of poetic pidgin—
and provoke all four of love and hope and trust and justice.
Your spirit now floats free on the wings
of birds in your emerald, gravid paradise.

Holding The Pillow

S.E. Street

Ryde Hospital 1979

It took me a week of working in the nursery before I realized all babies do not look the same. I wondered how much their features would change, what they would look like by the time they started school, as teenagers, as adults. I thought some had been woefully misnamed and hoped Beau and Fleur would grow into swans.

Sister Breen rapped her knuckles on the glass separating her office from the nursery, motioning me to her door.

'There's an adoption case in labour ward. Country girl. Fifteen. Do exactly what Sister Scott says.'

Both Sister Breen and Sister Scott ran their wards like boot camps. Army trained, they were renowned for bawling out young nurses.

In the delivery room, Sister Scott manoeuvred me into position, pushing a pillow into my chest. 'Your job is to hold this pillow so that she does not see the baby.'

The girl raised her head, taking in the pillow and then her eyes rose to mine. Her freckled face was rosy with exertion. Her mother stood beside her and as the girl pushed through another contraction, she bent down, their heads together, 'You're almost there, darling.'

As the baby slipped out, the girl leant sideways, trying to see around the pillow. The doctor cut the cord, Sister Scott enveloped the baby in white blankets, draping a final blanket across the top of the bassinet. With one hand on the bassinet, the other on my back, she propelled us both out of the room.

'What do we have?' Sister Breen asked.

'It all happened so fast,' I said, 'I'm not sure.'

'Well, you'd better find out.'

I unravelled the white cocoon. 'It's a boy.'

'Choose a name,' said Sister Breen, waving a slip of blue cardboard.

'Me?'

'Yes. It doesn't matter; it's only for a month. X-rays, blood tests, all have to be done. For bonding reasons, he has to have the same nurse. You're it. So, what's his name? Anything!'

'Timothy?'

'Timothy it is.'

When I was alone in the nursery, I bent my face down to smell the back of his neck. I wondered if I should have named him Cherub but then read that the biblical Timothy was the young Christian to whom Paul wrote, 'Let no man look down on your youth.'

On the third day, as I was lining the babies up in front of the viewing window for the relatives to admire, I saw her, hiding behind the crowd, dressed to go home. She met my eyes and stepped up to the window. I turned; Sister Breen was on the phone.

As I wheeled his bassinet down from the back of the room, her face, streaming with tears, stilled. She looked up at me, as if asking, *Is that really my baby? That perfect boy?* I nodded.

I heard Sister Breen rapping her knuckles on her office window behind me. By the time I turned back to the corridor, she was gone.

Born Again

Abby Partridge

When I was young, I would follow my mother as she made the beds, one after another. It was always early, just after my siblings had left for school, and the daybreak streamed through our east-facing windows, creating chequered patterns on the floorboards. I can still see the sheets billowing above my head, making the light swim with golden powder, catching me in the whirlwind, my arms outstretched as I tried to gather the sunshine into my pockets. Fairy-dust, I thought, sent from somewhere magical every morning.

I've started to think that maybe, up until not long ago, that's what I'd been doing my whole life—trying to catch sunshine, only to realise that in the shadows, it's all just dust.

When I left home for university, I slipped easily into a makeshift family so that I didn't miss my own. People crazy about saving the world. The back room of the church smelled like books and tea. I couldn't have imagined anybody feeling unwelcome there, not then. My favourite times were spent sinking into the ever-merciful couches with my friends, swapping sins for prayer and trying to explain how the world could hold so much pain and joy all at once. Enthusiasm bounced off the walls. We ate cake and sang songs and told each other how loved we were.

Keeping a secret is a tiring task. I had to name my sins, to keep the congregation happy: I swore, I lied, I lusted. Pray for me. For a little while, I could cover my tracks with such minor confessions. But months went by, and I realised that not even the god of the universe could change who I was: a woman wretchedly in love with a woman, with a future aching to be discovered rather than delayed within the chapel walls. I wasn't ready to confess when they found me out. And I wasn't allowed back that Sunday. Sunshine turned to dust.

Leaving was the hardest thing I've done. Though bitterness had begun to seep into the cracks that had been pried open, there were things I couldn't part with: my bible, read cover to cover and highlighted in all the right places; my journal, filled with unanswered questions and notes written in felt-tip pen; my guilt, swinging back and forth across my heart like a pendulum.

Some days my head still throbs with remorse and indecision. Is what I've gained worth the loss? An exposed secret, a faith left shattered. I know all the words to every hymn, but have no choir to sing with. I dream of purgatory, and long for heaven. I ache for the friends who turned their faces away from me, towards the pulpit.

Then there is comfort: she who loves me through my pain. There is gardening and writing. And when the tears come, and my breath catches, and the dust falls on shadowy ground, I just pray that god knows me better than I know myself.

My Son

Deborah Hellewell

Grieve is only a six letter word, how can it hold such weight?

My son did not lose his life in the car accident. It was just another ordinary day as I recall, a day just like any other day. However by this ordinary day's end every second of it would be indelibly etched in my mind, body and soul.

That phone call that every Mother dreads, those words, 'There's been an accident, a car accident, someone has died, someone else is clinging to life, please come to the hospital now.'

I can't, I live in a different state, I need to call someone, I need to book a flight, I need this to be a terrible dream . . . but it's not.

He is in the Intensive Care Unit. Will he be alive when I arrive? Please let me get to him in time, please.

He is *alive*. They lost him, then they brought him back. He is alive. Machines surround him; blood in, blood out, urine out, air in, air out, drains and drips, beeps and moans. He is broken, my boy is all broken.

I rush to his side. I want to gather him up in my arms and hold him tight to my heart, hold him tight and *never* let him go, but I can't. Instead I take his hand in mine; it's the only part of him that isn't broken.

'I'm here baby,' I whisper in his ear. 'Mummy's here and everything will be alright.' But nothing would ever be the same again.

Three months pass by in that hospital; months of nursing fractured and broken bones, hundreds of stitches, anxious moments. Will he walk? Maybehe won't ever walk again.

Slowly his physical injuries heal but his heart and soul will never heal. She is dead.

Never again will he gaze lovingly into her blue eyes, run his fingers through her golden hair, laugh or cry with her. Never again will her dazzling smile fill his days.

'I killed her mum; I was driving too fast in the rain.'

'It was an accident son, just a tragic accident.'

'No mum.'

'Yes son.'

'No.'

'Yes.'

'No.'

'*Yes, yes, yes, yes, yes*. Just a tragic accident.'

A decade has now passed by and still he grieves for her. I however grieve for my lost boy; my son who is alive in body only and only just as he now slowly destroys what's left of himself with Crystal Meth.

He can't bring her back I know that. What I don't know is if I can bring him back?

After

Robyn Osborne

My childhood is neatly fractured into two. Before; life is a warm cocoon, washed with a Sleeping Beauty haze. Then there is after. I look at photos of myself from that time and hardly know the lost, angry girl. For this is the beginning, when our family melts into nothingness.

The cane barracks are small and cramped, barely enough room for a family of five. Summer evenings are spent on the verandah, the screams of flying foxes mingling with the scent of bruised frangipani. When the broad sweep of the river is lit by the moon's glow, they watch for jumping fish, the silver forms arching above the dark waters. And always are their mother's words: family is everything.

One day their mother becomes ill and the children are scattered to other families. Life is strange and lonely, but they cope. This is only temporary, until she returns to them and they are a family again.

They drive to the hospital but can only see her for a short time. She is always so careful not to cry, to be brave and strong for them, but not this time. As she struggles to rise from the bed, wild with tears, hands outstretched, the despair gushes from her. Their father tries to calm her, but his shoulders sag. The children recoil. Their fear is palpable. Aunty gently moves them away and there is silence everywhere, except for her cries. They retreat to the park and spend time searching for ants in the grass. Searching for ants as their mother dies.

It is an ordinary school day when the neighbour comes for them. The children are driven silently to the minister's house, where they drink tea and nibble at cake in the morning sunshine. It is not until their father arrives, his eyes misted with grief that they understand. Quiet murmurings swirl in the air but no one says the words they dread—your mother is dead.

The funeral is on a day of beauty; glittering and bright with a high sad wind, as only autumn can be. Some dress in black but they choose colours. The youngest wears a skirt her mother made the year before. It sings of summer and life. In her clenched hands, bruised frangipanis, their scent forever tied to the fragility of love.

The 'after' has begun.

In the silence following her death, a slow anger burns. Shadows of pain sit hunched within the walls of the house, no longer a home. One by one they move away, haunted by the memory of the family they had once been.

I barely think back to that time of our greatest loss, when our world changed. The girl from my past is forgotten. Only I remain. Our barracks is long gone and the cane fields are choked by the glossy urban sprawl of thousands. Yet with the frangipani scent on a warm night, I know that the aching sense of loss will stay with me always.

Mourning Stone

Brenda Saunders

You have sent me a souvenir
from the frozen world
above the snowline

Rounded by time, ground down
by ice and glacial drift
the stone lies heavy
with the weight of loss

—memories of long nights
  landscapes black on white

Cold to the touch
its surface holds no sunlight

Pressed from some ancient tree
it warms against the skin
keeps a healing fire inside

When I Had A Secret

Barbara Kamler

im memoriam Leslie Jacobi

I set it on my friend's dining table
so she might see the contour of pain, the
depth of shame etched into its shadow.

With a gentle hand she lifts it, knowing
it has never been touched or held or heard
before—whispers so as not to frighten

it or let it fall to the floor, broken.
She waits for me to speak first, unpeeling
layers of loss onto the crimson cloth.

She listens and waits until it lies still,
coaxes it quietly to Redhead Cliff,
ocean pounding below, so it may hear

unknown melodies, breathe in the last shards
of sunlight—amid her melaleuca
and native banksia. On the walk home

she places it back in my hand. We go
in silence, graced by her witness, careful
stepping, the song of crickets at nightfall.

All In A Day

Lucinda Alynn

He wakes in the quiet hours before the sun rises, darkness still imposing itself through the uncovered windows. His hand creeps across the empty side of the bed; in her typical indecisiveness discarded clothes sprawled across her side. He hadn't even heard her alarm go off.

Rising from his own slumber, he begins the usual routine. A quick shower, shave and dress. His last freshly ironed shirt hang in the closet, saving the best for last: his wife's favourite. He always wore it on Fridays. His colleagues jokingly teased him on his fastidiousness.

Downstairs his two kids were up, attempting to get ready though barely old enough to wipe their own backsides. He hustled them along; tied their shoelaces, brushed their teeth; all the while Annie's perfume scented the house. She always wore more than was necessary, claimed she could never smell it. He smelt that perfume in his sleep. Dreamed of it.

He dropped the kids off at their grandmother's, kissed them goodbye and headed into work.

He sent Annie a text at lunch; asked about her day, said he loved her and would see her that night. He smiled at the picture on his desk, relishing in his sneaky theft. The one on her own, the one she hated, his favourite. His ugly mug nowhere insight.

Endless phone calls and meetings made the day go fast. His colleagues left him to his work.

He rang Annie on his way home. No answer. He mouthed along to her voice on the answering machine. *Beep.* 'On my way home babe,' he said, cheerfully.

The driveway housed his mother in law's car. Annie wasn't home yet.

Her scent still filled his nostrils the moment he walked inside. Their dog, Arnold sat faithfully in the same spot he always waited, tail wagging in elated anticipation.

'Not yet,' he whispered, generously patting the sad Labrador. He followed the playful screams of his three- and four-year-old down the hall. One setting the table, the other in her Nan's arms helping stir the boiling pot on the stove. He sat at his regular spot at the table, the kids rushing over to say hello. He ignored his mother in law's sympathetic greeting, instead questioning his wife's empty place at the table.

'Hey buddy,' he said to his son, 'You forgot a spot for mummy.'

They both glanced at their Nan. His little girl flushed.

'She's not comin' home daddy, 'member?'

He stared blankly at the girl who encompassed his wife's most flattering features. He nodded, stood up, walked past Arnold and up the stairs to his bedroom. His wife's clothes were still strewn across the spot she had left them, five weeks ago. He crawled into bed alongside them, set his alarm for the time Annie needed to be up; her own phone ominously lighting up with fifty two notifications of unanswered texts and calls.

He lay motionless, waiting for her haunting scent to return him to his beloved denial.

Marked Man

Linda Gooch

He wakes and the blanket has twisted around his body. When he loosens his arms one hand accidentally hits the brick wall and flakes the paint. The other hand grabs the blanket and throws it to the floor. He looks to the little window and its square of light. The sun outside sends shadows from the bars across the floor to the bunk. It stripes across his face, like a slow and deliberate slap. He prefers cloudy days when he can imagine he is somewhere else.

It's easier if he lies still. The first moments of remembering are the hardest. He hears the trolley coming down the corridor. A wheel squeaks. The clang of a door within a door. The tin tray into the slot. The squeaky wheel again. When it reaches his door he ignores it, as if this will make a difference. As if not noticing the meal shoved into his space gives him some control.

The trolley squeaks away.

The shadow lines have moved, beginning to angle across the wall beside him, creeping brick by brick. He does not look at the tray, not yet. Not until the memories are all back, crowded around him, pressing him down. He wants them locked in with him until sleep comes again.

He begins at the first words on the back of his wrist. Scratched with a blade, then rubbed with ink from a broken pen. It's faded blue with time, but the crude lines of a heart remain and the name of a girl. Fourteen was too young for love, the clumsy letters tell.

More ink brands the top of his arm. The blue-black barbed wire winds around his bicep, though now the points are blunt.

His chest, and the first coloured ink. Names this time, words that once spoke for him, pictures that had meaning.

The other arm twists with a viper. Its body rolls and coils along the muscle, its head rears at his forearm, its mouth is open and the fangs drip venom. This ink is crisp, the scales so realistic, the snake moves when he moves.

He brings his blue lettered knuckles together, as if pressing fist to fist can make them into something new, can push the good into the evil.

The room has filled with the crushing, noisy, strangling memories.

Almost there.

These are the hardest, the words he can only see in his mind. His fingers touch on the side of his throat. Here, he knows, is her name and two more. His fingertip hovers gently over them. Eyes closed now, he sees the delicate lines of the letters, the soft swirls and gentle curves. He sees his thick coarse fingers covering them.

A little further and his hand moves up to his cheek. He doesn't notice that it is wet. Moving from the corner of his eye he traces lightly with his finger down over his cheekbone.

Blue teardrops. One. Two. Three.

Fish Tank

Malcolm St Hill

You used to lift me up to the sky (Literally! Remember?)

The soft tap tap of your index finger
on the cylindrical rim.
The fine dark hairs on the back of your hand.
The smell of you as I sidle up close
for this daily ritual.

You have the rhythm now.
Autumn leaves fall with each tap
drifting apart on surface tension.

In the prism of the tank
water roosters with filament tails
plump comets
ascending hypotenuse
mouthing for communion
in the broken film.

Granular food
in the brother tank you gave me
before you left.
White-knuckle grip
hanging under the surface
drowning
sinking to the gravel below.

I am lost in that volume
sifting words at the bottom of the tank
crunching them like broken teeth
wanting to express to you now

my fear of losing you again.

No-One There

Pam Miller

He holds her hands and gazes at the wrinkled skin. So soft now. These hands haven't seen work in a long time. They are smooth and soft. Not like a baby's hand. All round and plump and strong and grasping and reaching out for new things . . . reaching out for life.

These hands are still. They are lined and wasted and weak. There is no purpose in their life. They don't cook or iron or clean or garden. They don't hug or touch or comfort.

That all stopped long ago.

It stopped when her 'confusions' started to appear, spreading its tentacles and stilling her hands. It forced the memories of her life into little recesses which could only be reached occasionally. In time, it pushed them further and further back. At first, it was every month when the memories couldn't be found. Then, every week. And then, every day. It left a huge black hole, where once a life full of love and laughter had been.

He turns her hand over. There is no resistance, no feeling, no recognition of his presence.

He strokes the hand that is so familiar and that he remembers so well. And he basks in the memories that these hands remind him of. His memories. Their shared memories.

He visits this empty shell of a person every week. He listens to the silence. He doesn't say much. She was always such a talker. 'Have a chat' was her nick name.

He grasps her hands and his memories of her. And he looks into the eyes of his mother. There is no one there.

Possessions

Hardeep Dhanoa

Death is the only guarantee in life, yet, it is always a shock when death makes his way to collect us. Sometimes people go knock on death's door themselves. My father was one of those people.

It is a beautiful Sunday morning when I wake to the sound of my sister screaming from my father's room. I ran in half asleep,

My sister is kneeling beside the bed sobbing, shaking uncontrollably.

My father is lying in his bed completely still, pale as the moon. He is in a deep, peaceful sleep.

I shake him.

'Wake up, wake up, wake up!' I plead.

No response. Dead.

On the bedside table is a bottle of pills and a neatly folded note which reads:

'Don't be sad my darling girls, some of us are not made for this world. It's cruel and everything I see is dark. I couldn't do it anymore, I couldn't do it. I want to see light, I want to be free. I'm sorry. Love always dad.'

My sister and I cry until nothing is left.

Since that moment life is a blur. The body is collected, there is a funeral and the bills stack up. This is all a nightmare and my dad is going to walk through the front door at any moment with my favourite of ice cream which we we're going to eat straight from the tub. I keep waiting for that moment and it never comes. I keep waiting for normality to arrive and it never does.

Sadness, anger and despair follow me, piercing me with pain.

Dad you were so selfish. Did you think about me? My existence does not make sense without you here. I get angry at myself for thinking he was selfish. He was in pain and I did not see it. Could I have done anything? I don't know what to think or what to feel. I wonder if the pain will ever go away.

Months pass and it's another beautiful Sunday morning and I finally have the courage to walk into my father's room. The bed is unmade, the glass of water still full, books stacked on the table, pictures hugging the walls, clothes scattered. All that is left of my dad are these things. This room is a shrine that is alive with memory. I read every book in the room, I play every record and in those moments I drift to a place where I feel an abundance of joy, a solace that hardly feels real. The sun shines its warmth through the window.

I hope he found light, so much light that his soul is forever illuminated in peace.

In this shrine my father lives and breathes.

He lives through me.

Black Holes

Patricia Bish

My beautiful, loving and eccentric husband, Robert, didn't believe in black holes. He found the latest idea of searching underground for 'dark matter' quite ludicrous.

'They've got it wrong. Black holes are simply cold matter,' he would declare. He even took a break from his metallurgical research to write a scientific paper about spiral galaxies in which he explained his theory mathematically.

I would like to tell him now that black holes do exist; that when I came home from church on St. Valentine's Day 2016—exactly forty-seven years since we were engaged—and discovered his beloved body lying lifeless under the drought-stricken trees on our property, I fell into the deepest and blackest hole, the bleakest void, in which I grope, not for dark matter, but for the shining star and dearest soul-mate that my Robert was and is for me.

Robert loved mathematics. When reports of violence and criminality, football scandals or political skull-duggery came flooding into our home via the television or radio, he would exclaim, 'Why don't they all stay at home and do mathematics!' Even when we were out socialising, he would bring out his pencil and paper and, professor-like spectacles poised on the bridge of his nose—methodically start jotting down his latest equations.

But powerful as they may be, mathematical equations won't bring him back to me or solve the agonising enigmas of life and death; the sudden extinguishing of a vibrant intellect—loving, humorous, wonderfully complex, with such a rich store of accumulated wisdom to offer the world—blown out like a candle in the wind.

I said that he was eccentric and he was, but in such an endearing, if sometimes irritating, way: wiping everything religiously with methylated spirits, especially the seats of chairs after guests had departed: cutting the plastic rings around bottles because of his horror of death by hanging: trying to avoid hand-shaking and public toilets. . . the list goes on. A couple of years ago, when one equally quirky chap suggested bowing as an alternative to hand-shaking, he was delighted. He and the chap practised bowing to each other and managed to hit their heads together.

At home, he would often scuttle around surreptitiously with his meths bottle so as not to upset me and would grin self-consciously, like a guilty schoolboy, if I caught him. Then we would both chuckle and sometimes hug each other. His innate intelligence and sense of humour would always redeem him from the black holes of obsession.

Black holes do exist, Robert. Life without you is infinitely dark matter for me. I cannot fathom a way forward without you and see only a long dark tunnel ahead. I can only pray, in defiance of all scientifically bleak logic, that, somehow, at the end, you will be there to greet me with your heart-achingly dear and loving smile, proving that a black hole is indeed cold matter—merely the frozen zone where love must hibernate before summer returns.

Ponga (Silver Fern)

Janette Hoppe

again—
the day is not flowing easily
and forcing it never seems to work

the sky is falling,
darkness settling in for the night
I watch with heavy eyes
the hours ticking by
I guess this is called moving on

I hate the way my stomach flattens when I lay on my back
the rare creeping
my womb can only remember
the way it felt
the slow growing fern
the unexpected unfurling frond
reaching out
then recoiling before it had the chance to grow

the lost beep on the machine
the white noise,
the silver light,
'no heart beat'
was all I heard
before the night rolled in

And What Happens Next?

Kym Milne

Another night with no sleep so I lay and watch the sky lighten. In the midst of all this mess and heartache there is beauty in this one small moment. Had I drifted into sleep his large hands would have slapped me hard awake. These same hands haul me off into depths of sorrow and unimaginable suffering and these big hands also cradle all of my shaking hurts.

He offers no peace and he can match my hopelessness on every level. I have grown so used to him and the daily savagery he inflicts that I cannot imagine my life without him. He came to me so unexpectedly in a terrible moment that tore at my heart and robbed me of all hope and my, once quiet, gratitude. He said he knew exactly how I felt. That there was no one else who could ever understand what I was going through but him. He dissected every wound to show that I needed to entrust him and him alone with all of my pain. And I do!

He will huddle next to me under the sheets stroking my sob racked body and my unwashed hair. He is the keeper of my darkest thoughts. At times he is unkind but he is also the gentle one to wipe my unrelenting tears. He tells me, too, that to have a gaping hole in my heart is perfectly okay just as it is permissible to believe I will never be happy again. He has tethered my bruised soul to his in such a way I fear I have become someone I no longer recognise and, for that alone, I do not even care.

When my pain is sharp, unbearably deep, I cling to him. He is my support and my comfort and in moments, when I believe all courage has surely been lost to me, he is there. He has come to know me better that I know myself and I accept his rightful place in my life. Grieve, it would seem, has a mighty powerful hold over me.

But I am also waiting. I do not tell Grieve, but, I am quietly awaiting Forgiveness for she, in her beauty, wisdom and truth, will confess the cruelty of all suffering and heartache so brutally inflicted. Although she is just out of my reach I know she is there and my belief is that we will eventually unite. Forgiveness will be my freedom from Grieve and, unlike formidable Grieve, she will be kind with her words when she says, *'You are braver than all of your heartache. Although you deserve to feel this terrible anguish and sorrow you also deserve they not destroy you.'*

With her gentle encouragement, we will cut my ties with Grieve; shut him from my life along with Sadness and Darkness who Grieve revels in the company of. And what happens next? Well that's a new beginning for us all.

Tending The Memory of Two Sisters

Kathyrn Fry

i
The whorls of petals, pearl-white, beckon
—a curve here, a fullness there, one
part-hidden, a layer reaching—like her stories:

Land Army Girls, rations for petrol, oranges
and sugar, sewing shirts, knitting socks for war,
the unravelling of '45.

In her teens as steady home-help, she missed a career.

Later she married, had sons, weathered uphill
days of shearing, harvest and fires, drawing
solace from Church and town.

She travelled to us and we to her by inland hills lit
with Salvation Jane, her mothering arms open,
her hands folding our moments.

The rose we tend in memory of her is long-stemmed
and fragrant, though she wasn't tall
                                and seldom wore scent.

ii
Two cats in the doorway, one cleans the other.
Velvet drapes, leather chairs, Bach in the room.

She spins, weaves and knits, fashions bears
from sheepskins—a character for each new kin.

For their bed-ridden father, she resigned
to turn him over six years, every few hours.

She shows me a gown for an unknown bride
(the light fall of her fine-wool crochet),

and her table mats, her tatting of fractals.
She hands us eight. Now I can die, she laughs.

Each visit she gives us feijoas, our car full
of heady scent for the long trip home.

The tree we grow to honour her now
has yet to bear such fruit.

House On The Hill

Sarah Moriarty

That house on the hill. Snuggled contently in the bush, in a green nook at the base of the mountain. You were happy there, in your wellington boots and sun-hat; tending your garden, feeding the ducks. You took such joy in simple beauties that you sparkled, radiating light into even the dullest of days. My vivacious friend, who would go to any lengths to make me smile, to give me confidence.

Did I abandon you?

I'm not sure when it all changed. Things seemed to weigh you down. Even you didn't know why. Hard days began to assault your senses, insult your character. Your light dwindled. All the while a quiet assassin was waiting, lurking. A dark presence around every corner, always felt, but never seen.

Did I abandon you?

I would take calls, teary and long, be that strong shoulder that you had, so many times, been to me. I told you I'd watched the beauty of a flickering candle one night; how it had wavered, buffeted by the breeze but never extinguished. Hospital visits. Bunches of flowers. Cooking. Being. And those calls, teary and long.

Did I abandon you?

One by one, they dropped like wilted blooms; friendships, withering and falling.

Pills. Booze. Accidents. Hospitals. Flowers. Friends. Round and round went the merry go round. I tired. You tired.

My own light started to dim. I'd been angry. In denial. Bargained. I would take your calls; encourage, support. But I was mourning my lost friend. You sensed it too. You let me go.

Exhausted, I'd abandoned you.

And one night, at that pretty house on the hill, you took those pills as you so often had done before. But you didn't make the call, that final call for help that had saved you so many times before. Had you decided it was time? Or did you just leave it too late? Why, why?

I wasn't there. None of us were there. The spark of our exquisite friend, which had once shimmered and glittered, flickered and went out. And I wasn't there.

There you lay. Finally at peace, at your lovely little house on the hill. For days. And we didn't know.

What I wouldn't give to change it. To change me. To shake you awake, cradle you, make that call for you. To fight for you. For you to know you could call me and it would be okay. Even if we became strangers. Just to know that your beautiful light was still sparkling away, at your house on the hill.

Nine Years Gone

Julie Watts

I do not miss you everyday   but I do.

the sun is on the paperbarks
their feet   in winter water

silky webs   stretch from rough bush
to rough bush   shining lines of diamond

the dog is skittish   with ghosts
baulks at shadows   angular shapes

the grass turns lime in the light
and the scuffing path   sighs

wild lilies   catch at my legs as I pass
and crows hop   under the ancient olive

reeds are riddling   the still dark pond
my hand   on the thick thatched waist of Tuart

ducks sunk   into their afternoon snooze
wear your colours

nine years on   and still words scarcely come
inadequate always   to outline your absence.

the children are growing   into their
genetics of you

developing their legacies
taking their place   in the linage

history holds them   as it holds you
not as ash   caught and buried in some

blank box   but living   in the bone
and flesh   blood and sweat of them

as they struggle   unfold   in their ripening
existences
you are all over them—
I do not think of you every day   but I do

in the sun   its hash of light   and shadow
on the path ahead   where the dog dashes

nine years gone
I do not miss you every day   but I do.

Hoarder

Lynne Evans

When the house became too dusty too dirty too much too many, your car became pantry office wardrobe. McCain's frozen dinners, Tim Tams, melted, Daliesque. Christmas gifts your arms couldn't bear inside—a gold movie pass, a travel case, a diary for 2016. Macca's containers with one wizened fry, a ripped-open packet of plastic cutlery, a Peter Alexander nightie with Superman on the front. Mintie wrappers, ants mummified in their creases. Three and a half pairs of shoes, a CD of *Waiting for Godot*, year eleven essays, eleven bulging tins of Dine, the sunglasses you lost last year and another two pairs. Eight dollars sixty five in coins, coated in hair and something else. Permission notes for an excursion to the Seymour Centre and one white elbow-length glove. On the floor leaves had gathered, resting with some crumpled notes you'd written to yourself. My phone number, which you knew by heart, on one. The petrol tank half-full.

O my lovely, scruffy, grubby, glamorous friend. I wish I could hoard you still. I would keep your laughter, the way you had of cackling with your eyes. Those times we couldn't look at each other in meetings for fear of breaking into the unstoppable. Your long, expressive, expansive arms, the silver bangle you had cut off because it annoyed some kid doing an exam. The way you tried to walk like a model and ended up looking like someone trying to walk like a model. Hair curly, unruly, shining—until. That scuffed black wallet bursting with receipts and notes, bulging with generosity. The music: *Renee Fleming, Chopin, Gladys Knight, Purcell.* 'Make sure you listen to it properly.' Articles, reviews, poems, you'd rip from magazines, even books and send to me. Those cats. Only in the last months were they fed anything but chicken or steak. You dressed them in old sets of dolls' clothes. They scratched you and hid from everyone else. The Hills Hoist was used to hang gobbets of meat for the magpies. We talked about one day playing havoc racing our wheelchairs in the corridors of some unfortunate nursing home. There was not time. You could shock me but I couldn't shock you. Now you've left me. Shocked and dented and sad.

I Live With Disability

Annabel Hallett

A diagnosis. Is it good or bad? Seven years but only four with me. Seven years of appointments and no answers. Four years of reminders; I wish you knew me before. Before this insidious monster dug its claws in.

It's not cancer, it's not cancer, I remind myself. God I hope we get an answer. Something we can grab, something we can fight.

The doctor speaks, the answer comes. Was it the answer I feared most, the answer we prayed for?

'An aggressive form,' he says, 'the form with all the extras you don't want.'

Does its name give it life or make it manageable? How long before wife becomes carer? How much pain will there be? Will the medication slow it down? Questions, so many questions.

I live with disability but it is not my own. I live with fear and anger. Why did this happen to me? But it did not happen to me, it is not my physical battle, I am only a bystander. I look at the fractured dream of our future—the ifs, the buts and the whats? This is not my disease, I should not feel scared or sad or angry. He needs me to be positive. He needs me to support him. Doesn't he? I need him to need my support because without that I am living with disability but I am suffering alone.

I live with disability. The future I planned is gone but the future I have unwittingly chosen is here. The man I love is here. But we are living with disability. It is slow, quietly strangling him. It rears its ugly head but only he can see it. I watch a one sided battle. It eats at him, striking again and again. Yesterday it missed, today its dagger-like teeth find their target. Tomorrow it misses again, but only just. I grapple with anxiety as I wait for the next assault. How long will this one last? Each puncture takes small pieces of him.

'I wish you had known me before,' his voice is frustrated.

But I did know you before, I want to scream. *I knew before this. I have seen the changes.*

The spoken and unspoken losses hangs in the air like a spider webs. Invisible and sticky, we mustn't get caught. We mustn't feed the monster.

I live with disability, it is not my loss, it is not my disease but it is my grief.

Sketch Of A Man

Jo Lyons

Tellingly, there are few photos including both Dad and me. My baptism. A group shot at the beach where I'm a rudie-nudie sitting on the sand and Dad's in budgie smugglers—not our finest hour. The picnic where we both rock our best Seventies hair. A couple form a series: Baby Drinks Dad's Beer.

He exists in outline. In photos. In objects, symbols of a life—his architectural plans, pencils, his books, his drawings, ties, dressing gown. In stories told to keep his memory—or my memories of him—alive. My scant memories, which may only stem from other people's: half-remembered dream fragments. From this distance it's hard to discern their truth.

I remember Mum taking me upstairs to the den to say goodnight. Dad lifted me to touch the ceiling—that giddy feeling of being raised by big hands while my little ones reach high. Sometimes he spun me around on his stool at his drafting table, or maybe drew pictures on my hand. There is the faint wisp of smoke, rough whiskers as he nuzzles my cheek or blows raspberries on my belly.

I remember sitting at the dining table, most siblings present, air heavy with tension. Someone wouldn't eat their dinner or was naughty and got in trouble off Dad, and it was scary. But there are special baked dinner memories, and birthdays with cake that had a ballerina on top. Picnics at Cordeaux dam, going to Dad's work Christmas parties, long car rides to family gatherings, running around parks. Pretending to be a princess and living in a castle with my family, happily ever after.

Our last shared photos are at my eldest sister's wedding, group shots of our big family—the happy couple, my sisters a row of real-life princesses in Laura Ashley lace. Mum smiling, Dad gaunt but proud, his suit too big. A few people look down at me, the grumpy four-year-old flower girl chewing her fingernails.

In my mind the house quickly became quieter. Dad was in bed a lot and sometimes we were allowed to see him. Standing in the doorway to Mum and Dad's bedroom, not sure what to do; you have to be quiet. Visitors came and I was shy.

Then I have a glimpse of me at home, sitting on the brown carpet in our dining room, my white-stockinged legs tucked under me, and I smooth my good black and white checked dress over my knees. I'm in a patch of warm sun; light streams through the window and catches on dust motes floating through the air. Sitting primly, basking in the feeling of a nice dress and polished shoes, being a big girl, though kind of uncomfortable. There's a buzz of activity around me and I'm trying not to be in the way, not to be noticed by these strangers. I sit there waiting for my family to come home from church. I'm told it was overflowing with people wanting to say goodbye.

When Your news

blinked blue on my phone
I fell back to feel my heart again.

Thumbing through each pained line,
I kept thinking, funny how we've gone
back to reading in scrolls.

I kept picturing you frozen in the doorway,
lashed by the streaming sun not quite

reaching the bed where she lay, as it hit you,
dark and earth-heavy, that the silence,
the silence was all your own.

You tried to pummel the beat back into her heart,
fighting off the blackness pulling you to her.

But the finality this time, this last time you couldn't
pull her back. And I kept hearing this gasping wail
thinning into blinding white screams.

Later when we talked, as you lamented for her mum,
clad in orthodox black and guilt-lit prayer,

was it too crass that I could hear blue rembetika
and kept wondering whether you would also
cry for yourself, then and there?

I wanted then to pull you through the phone,
pull the pain out of you, pull you close,

and I was sure I could hear, or wanted to,
discarded rage tamped down hard
in the midden of your grief.

Ignatius Kim

The Silent Man

Dan Archer

The world isn't for everyone. Some thrive, some survive and others stand still as life shifts around them in a hastened blur, breathing from one day into the next. And some possess hearts that cannot climatise to the bitter chill of reality, visiting graveyards in their minds, whereupon they walk between rows of faded dreams, decaying memories, fears and consequences.

I once knew a man like this. He was a husband, father, teacher, friend, and a man armed with a stand-off wit and a discerning smile. To know him was to admire the rhythmic order of his life, packaged neatly into the suburban dream. You made it real, wearing your smile as an alibi.

What happened, friend? Did the revolving cycle of the suburban grindstone wear you down? You chased your shadows too far, colliding, they ranaway inside of you. What did your eyes see that others could not?

I remember your eyes, sharp and blue. Your face stern in deep rumination would melt away into animated fires of smiles and laughter. But always sharp and blue were your eyes. They seemed to pass right through me as if your thoughts were floating just beyond my head. They removed you from yourself. They told the story of you.

In the life you left behind, I understand you better now. Propriety is a narrow path to walk, and you were playing a part. Your consciousness faltered upon the stoic truth that free will is fatally limited and bound up tight in convention.

How did you house it? No cracks to expose your polished shell, you seemed whole and steady. Someone to be counted upon. Somehow you pinned it down, never showing your wounds. It must have been like trying to hold air underwater with your hands.

When I heard the news about you, it was early. Like you I too became still, paralysed by the sobering cold of loss. Time gusted around me in a blur of colour and ritual. The world became peripheral that day as I watched my hands follow their old paths where my thoughts could not. It wasn't until I arrived home that I read the news with my own eyes. The lingering possibility of false hearsay snuffed out into a twist of smoke, whirling skywards to lay with you. The symptoms of grief, a lament for the downtrodden.

Was it salvation you found at the bottom? Or the quick eclipse of the end? I hope that when the rocks rose up to catch you, that your fears vanished into the flash of black. I hope that in your rest, you dream back over your time and see yourself as you were. Loved.

Goodbye.

On Leaving

Lawrence Bernard

I lost my father and my wife at the same time. He died and she moved out.

When my father died it was a relief. 'Old Timers' Disease' put down by a cancerous colon. For me, his funeral wasn't sad, having grieved at every stage of his slow descent into delirium until only detritus remained, like dry leaves in the cobwebbed corners of an empty shed, its unhinged door flapping in the wind.

For three years my father's shed lay abandoned; robbed of those things that made him Dad. The thieves would come in the night and the mower would be missing, then the potting mix, the old printing press and the radio. All that remained were echoes of Johnny Cash and the jangle of car keys and burps and farts and his familiar growl. I watched over him during those years and waited for him to die, but there's no dying with dignity when you have dementia. I knelt before his low hanging fruit untangling his skinny, white legs from his underpants. I pulled chocolate from his mouth still wrapped in foil. I took him on shuffling, oblivious walks around the garden, pointing out the things he once loved. And I stopped taking my kids to visit when they grew afraid.

The leaving is so glacial, it's hard to find the right way to say goodbye. Too early and he thinks you're pushing him out the door. Too late and your left staring at that abandoned shed. I guess I started saying goodbye, started grieving, when I first realised he was leaving. Imagine autumn if there were no spring. Long before Dad died, I recall sitting in the car with my young son and allowing him to see me cry. It seemed important.

When my wife left that too was a relief, mostly because I couldn't do it myself. Again, it took a while and I grieved in increments as our marriage slowly died. Looking back, there were lots of little watershed moments tinged with cold certainty. The separation started small and ended in a chasm so vertiginous that it paralysed me. First the talking stopped, then other privileges like sharing the bed or seeing her naked. For years I rode a rollercoaster, holding on and letting go until finally I stood staring at another abandoned shed that echoed the artefacts of a past life.

Divorce itself isn't that difficult, it's really just the bill after the burial. But the separation from my kids was a gut wrenching, chest crushing pain that permeated everything. 'It's Fathers' Day,' they chime and the embers glow in the furnace. Damocles' sword pierces my ribs and Thor's hammer pounds it relentlessly against a black anvil sitting hard and heavy inside my chest, driving home a constant reminder that every day is Fathers' Day.

There are rooms in my mind where memories reside, but some still pace the corridors of my life's lament for loved ones leaving.

Unlucky Thirteen

Elise Hassett

I was having a shower when I found out.

There was a hesitant knock on the bathroom door before it opened, just a crack. I assume Dad popped his head in far enough to deliver the news, but I couldn't really see him through the steamed, opaque glass; I could only hear his disembodied voice.

'Mum's died,' he said, without ceremony or emotion.

'OK,' I replied, in much the same way.

And just like that, it was over.

All her treatments—the surgery, the radiotherapy, the pain relievers, the vitamins, the raw foods, the juices, the brown rice, the steamed vegetables, the wholemeal *everything*, the meditation, the relaxation, the optimism, the *fight*—had amounted to nothing. Nine months of hopes tempered by setbacks, now finished.

Cancer had won.

I cried because I knew that was what I was supposed to do, but not because I felt anything. I was empty. With eyes closed, I let the water run in hot streams over my face and shoulders, rinsing me, before disappearing down the plughole, taking my crocodile tears with it.

I don't remember stepping out of the shower. I don't remember drying myself, or getting dressed. I don't remember anything else from that day, except playing Monopoly with my grandfather. He was at our house, but I don't know how he got there or even when he arrived.

Birthday

Timothy Higgins

Lights glimmered dimly on the windshield. Specs of pink and gold danced through dribbling rain, kissing each other and becoming part of a larger whole. Robert sat brooding in the back seat. He was twelve. His sister, Emily, four, squeezed his hand and sobbed. In front of them beer cans clanked and their father hiccuped. His knuckles were white. The leather wheel groaned underneath them as he wrestled the heavy Commodore down the road. He tried to keep the car in a straight line.

He couldn't.

Robert watched the back of his father's head. Waiting, praying. His father mumbled under his breath. Emily sobbed louder.

'Robert, shudderup!' His father swerved up the winding mountain-road, tyres wailing, and bashed the wheel with a fist. Robert placed a hand on his sister's head and kissed it gently. Her sobs softened and she nuzzled her brother's chest. Robert closed his eyes, Emily closed hers, and their father drove them deeper into darkness.

It was well past midnight and Robert tried to sleep. When he closed his eyes he heard his mother screaming. He heard meaty bashing and his father shouting and wanted nothing more than to die. He looked down. Emily snored softly in his lap.

He had taken off her seatbelt.

'It hurts.' She had complained.

'Robert! Help her.' His father's eyes appeared in the rear view mirror. Bloodshot and ugly.

'But—'

'Do as I say you stupid shit.'

Robert did as he was told.

In the distance the sky was turning a silvery blue. Birds chirped and leaves flittered through the windy valley below. Emily snored softly.

No.

Not Emily.

Glass shattered and metal groaned as the hulking vehicle bit into the tree and tumbled over the cliff. For a split second Robert saw the whole forest stretched out before him. His stomach sank and he closed his eyes.

Then his seatbelt pulled him down.

Robert's head was thrown to the side and his brow opened against the door frame. His ears rang and vomit filled his mouth as shards of glass kissed grooves into his cheek. The world flipped end over end and some-where beyond his eyelid's Robert heard a little head thumping around the cabin. The car stopped near the base of the valley, caught against a tree. He sobbed into his shirt as he wiped away the blood.

He picked up his sister and held her. She was limp. Pale blue eyes staring blankly into the sunroof. Robert gripped her. Waiting, praying. Frozen. Her head was cracked wide open. The contents soaked into the back seat. Robert watched the back of his father's head, rested gently against the airbag.

Snoring.

Above them light glimmered dimly through the leaves. He was twelve.

She was only five.

The Hole

P.S. Cottier

The hole in the corner scratches small holes with six legs
The hole rises from the corner and leans on my legs
The hole senses that I am crying and licks my hand
The hole takes advantage of my distraction and steals a sandwich
The hole eats its toothsome booty faster than any crocodile
The hole looks dismayed at sudden, unwarranted criticism
The hole decides that I need a game and grabs its rubber duck
The hole minces around the lounge room with a duck-shaped green tongue
The hole contains all sleekness and fatness and manic energy in the world
The hole evades my stretched hand and takes its duck to the corner
The hole settles down on its mat with the duck near its yawning mouth
The hole fades into its holeness, and my hands stroke mere memory
The hole in the backyard holds the bones of the one who has become the hole
The hole responds to its name, one further time, and an inexorable tail sweeps the air
The hole rises, weightless, and goes to wherever such lovely creatures must go
I clutch a mat, and survey hairy floors, bowl, and a limp green rubber duck

To My Son

Liz Fletcher

Sometimes people ask me how I got out of bed the day after you died. Of all the questions about death and dying, they ask me this. Would I have asked the same question once? I don't think so. I think I would have wanted to know how they learnt to live with the 'foreverness' of death, and knowing that their loved one would never walk through that door again. How they coped with the reality that at every celebration for the rest of their lives one person will be missing. How they related to the normalness of life where people complain about seemingly trivial things. How they controlled the paralysing fear for the safety of their other children. I like to think that I would have sat a while and talked about their child, their memories, their hopes and dreams and what they have lost.

I can never be sure though as that moment did not occur. Now I am writing this with the hindsight of knowing these are some of the important questions a bereaved parent struggles with.

I want to tell people that when you died I lost a chunk of my past, my present and my future. My dreams, I discovered, were woven with strands of you. The tapestry that was being created of our lives can never be finished as the thread is no longer available. You are my first thought every morning and my last thought every night. I want to say that the pain I felt when you died was physical as if someone had taken a scalpel to my heart and carved out a Luke shaped hole. I live with a dichotomy of despair and joy, I never realised the human heart could hold such contradictory feelings at the same time. When I watched your brother graduate from school I was swamped with emotions; his happiness at his sense of accomplishment and expectations of what lay ahead for him made my heart swell with love and joy. At the same time I was reminded that you would never have these experiences or be able to share in your brothers' special days either. I want to tell them that the pain I carry is not just for me, it's for your brothers too, but mostly it's for you. It's for all the things you will never get to do again or for the first time. You will never get to dance in the rain again, or feel the warmth of the sun on your back. You will never experience the anticipation of your first date, or your first kiss. You will never get to wait at the end of the aisle as you watch the love of your life walking towards you. You will never get to hold your newborn child for the first time and feel that overwhelming sense of love for him or her. I want to tell people all of these things, but they never ask..

A Text Message And Seven Kilometre Walk

Rosanna Garland

There it was
your message on my phone
he died in his sleep last night

you said he died peaceful
in his wife's arms
but such condolence didn't make it better

I let it settle on the screen
I expected it to brew or breed
what was I to say?

I take myself and the phone for a walk
seven kilometers to be exact
what was I to say?

I start to write *I'm sorry*
but I may as well tell you
of the weather

It is a windy Canberra August
your dad liked the cold
and probably wanted to leave with it

I cannot think of more to write
your father has no need now
for words, a phone
or seven kilometre walks

and then the phone again
thinking it was you, I answered

a friend's husband
a baby had been born

I don't know what to say
the footpath froze my joggers
my phone still felt like a gravesite

death and birth came
on a seven kilometer walk
and I still had no words but the weather.

Thread

Kerrie-Lee Guest

Blood curdled around the plug hole. Sticky, black hair was caught in its trap. A long needle floated in the crimson. Line upon line of red thread poured from her into the dingy water.

The children gathered at her feet. They grabbed at her and held her in their sticky, scrawny fingers. Oh how she loved them. She longed to enjoy them. She longed to dress them up in ribbons and bows. She longed to buy them sweet treats.

She watched their ruddy faces as she threw potato peels and rabbit scraps into the pot. Their clothes were clean but small. One thread hung from the bottom of Hettie's dress, holding her attention. She knew it would not last the rest of the winter.

Dinner was noisy and there was the thrilling trickle of children's laughter despite the meagre offering. Her husband had arrived home early. Once again his daily trip to the wharf for work went unrewarded. But she smiled and tried to ignore the sweat building on her forehead and the nausea swelling from deep within. She engaged with her loves on the accounts of the cricket game in the neighbour's yard. She relished their stories of corn cob cars that raced each other across the road. She spoke in soft reprimand to the grimy, well-worn doll responsible for Lily's lost marble.

The children squirmed as she tucked them into bed. They complained that the blanket was scratchy. That Mary was hogging the bed. That Lily would snore. That Hettie still wet the bed. Her husband, soft and gentle, soothed their whines with a kiss to the top of each head.

Her breathe caught in her throat but she struggled on, trying to mend another shirt. The rash spread over her face, red and sweaty despite the decided chill in the night air. The sickness swelled but she held a spark in her eye as she recalled holding her babes in her arms. In another world, another life, she would have filled a grand home with teams of children.

Her husband called to her but she had nothing left in her to respond. He knew nothing of her sacrifice, but that was her choice, her choice to avoid burdening him further. It was not her choice to be fading away.

Her eyes fluttered as in her mind she saw herself pushing a new child in a pretty stroller . . . she was watching her lovely, little boy in a hand-made swing from the fig tree in the yard.

It all felt so tangible, so real.

And in her last moments she knew that in trying to kill one to save them, she had destroyed them all.

Blood still lingered in the tub with the knitting needle whilst the blood left inside turned against her. Her sewing fell from her hand and she left her place quietly.

Somewhere she held her new baby in her arms.

Untitled

Judith Pugh

Now I can contemplate the scalpel
Making the cut into your fragile skin
Something about the stillness of your body
Resists the thought of bone and flesh within

I worry though so many years have gone now
That you were warm when they began to strip
Whatever bits and pieces that they wanted
Your tiny heart, your thymus gland, a slip

Of something for the microscope to ponder
While I lay alone and longing for your touch
Dreading the incinerator wondered
Where you were buried.

Hoping for too much.

Night Swim

Jill O'Meara

(For David J. Marks)

We stole
into the city's gardens
and giggling ourselves
over a spiked fence I
tore my underwear
we laughed so much
we nearly died

then

inhaling the harbour's
salty breath, we
rolled on night—
jewelled lawns
for hours
we were outlaws,
midnight fabulists
renaming flowers
after friends;
all the beautiful
young men

while

above us flying foxes fluttered
like black handkerchiefs.

I broke into the pool
clinging to the harbour,
next to the gardens
after your wake,
gliding in the dark—
for hours.
Remembering
all the names.

Above me flying foxes fluttered
like black handkerchiefs.

Sterile

Tyler Eli

I feel shock gnawing inside me. I sit down outside the doctors rooms for a moment. I want so badly to cry, but I do not want to be seen. I need to get home. Home seems so far away. I could catch a taxi. It would be quicker. If I do, it will be at least twenty dollars. More than I can afford to spend. Especially now. It will have to be a bus, but do I stop for a coffee first? I would love a fresh frothy cappuccino, but how long can I contain the tears? Tears looking for an avenue of escape. I focus on my breath and pull myself up on my feet. I will catch the bus and make the short walk home. I can make myself a cup of coffee at home. Then if I cry it will be hidden from the public. I count the steps inside my head, one, two, no eye contact, three, four, just keep walking, five, six, nearly there, seven. There is nowhere to sit but that's ok. I am happy to stand and wait. Wait for the bus to take me home. Home to safety. Home to contemplate, and cry.

I check the answering machine as I walk in the door. No message. The crying starts and continues into sobs. Time of no importance, the tears flow free and steady. I have no one now. No one to listen or offer advice. No one to be there to hold my hand. No one there for me. It has been two months since Ben left and I have not heard a word from him. I check my answering machine, not only when I arrive home, but also when I come in from the garden, or get out of the shower. Nothing. I never had the chance to tell Ben about the little person that has lived inside me. The minute being that introduced me to the toilet bowl on a regular basis. The butterfly flutters inside my belly that excited me. The little person that I was waiting to meet one day. The being, which for a brief period of time, distracted my thoughts from the biological clock. Tick, tock, tick, tock.

Tomorrow I will go to the hospital. I will have this person taken from me. One final ultrasound to confirm before they sedate me. I am angry. Angry because I am almost forty. Angry because Ben will never know about the person we created together. Angry because our baby's heart stopped it's rhythmic beat. The beat so fascinating to hear. Like a tom tom drum. Rhythmic, hypnotic, perfect. Tomorrow I will lose my baby in the same sterile environment I expected to deliver it in. Not in this way. Not like this. Empty and alone.

Bequeath Me This

Nicola Moorhouse

He spends most of his time in the corner of the room sitting quietly, neither seen nor heard. When I first got him he clung to my back, squeezing my temples with his large leathery hands, clamping them so firmly it felt like my skull was going crack. Now he hovers in the corner, silent and dark, contemplating.

I know he is there. Always visible to me like a gloomy shadow in my peripheral vision. His constant presence lulls me. Everything is calm, everything is still. Like a beautiful ocean lake that beckons you in whilst concealing the tiger sharks that circle at its depths.

On sunny days he moves towards the window. He stands beneath the sill with his cold breath forming condensation on the glass, distorting the view and making it impossible to see through.

Some nights I cannot sleep. He sits on my chest forcing me awake. Struggling to catch my breath as his weight bears down on my solar plexus with so much presure, I think my ribs might cave in.

It was not a gift; he was bequeathed to me on my best friend's death bed. She's gone now. She left me with this.

A Life Of Birds

Alison Gorman

Somewhere in Russia, a great grey owl
rests in a larch tree listening
for lemmings burrow beneath snow.
Her head swivels like a radar,

sweeping the quiet for sound.
In South Africa, a lanner falcon
turns in the sky, scanning the plains
for sparrows. Black onyx eyes

narrow as she plucks her prey from flight.
You, lover of birds watch them glide
on TV and forget you're here,
lying upon a new bedspread, patterned

with forest and fern. White hair, soft
and washed. Thin legs lost in the beige
folds of your trousers. Still, except
for the short, quick rises of your chest.

We marvel at bee hummingbirds
in the woodlands of Cuba. Tiny, iridescent
connoisseurs sip nectar from red flowers
with rapid wings and hearts.

But later, you tell me apostle birds
crowd your back step in grey suits
waiting for grain, like bookies in the ring
while you pull on boots and plait

a new thong for your whip. Magpies
patrol your silver beet in glossy
tuxedoes pulling grubs after rain.
Blue wrens (those cornflower bandits)

hop and chit amongst the poplars
that line your driveway and willy wagtails
hitch jaunty rides on the backs of sheep.

In the furthest paddock, wedge tail
eagles nest high in the redgums
and watch you mend fences.
They soar without wing beat
in the thermal currents of noon.
But it is the teal ducks, you admire
from your battered, blue ute.
How they rise from the channel at dusk
like a perfect chord, as you drive

your way home.

Grandmother's Clothes, 1-7

Gillian Telford

Chung Shun-Wen, 2009 gouache paintings
White Rabbit Gallery, Sydney

Through ritual, you find her; your fingers rub paint,
stir mineral pigments into a binder.
Her fingers once lifted and folded her clothes,
lingered to smooth each shirt and cheongsam.

From pigments worked through gelatin binders
soft colours emerge, like rain-washed blossom,
as soft as the shades of her shirts and cheongsams,
their silks, fine cottons, age-worn and thin.

With muted colours, like celadon, ivory,
you paint her clothes just as she left them, still
folded in drawers; raw silks and brushed cottons,
hand-stitched pockets, rows of pearl buttons.

You paint her clothes the way you found them;
shade collars and cuffs, the satin finish
of corded pockets, the tiny buttons she
fumbled to grasp with age-slowed hands.

Yet still she straightened collars and cuffs
as her fingers lifted and folded her clothes.
You saw her hands become stiff and slow—
through ritual you find her, your fingers in paint.

note:
eastern gouache paints or 'glue-colour' are made by mixing mineral pig-
ments into a gelatin binder.

The Car, The Boxes

Karen Throssell

not thinking of Pandora
you speak of the car, the boxes
not thinking of what would crawl out:

death dragged out of safe abstraction
by his own hand no longer a flourish
I see that hand taking the hose, stealing
the pills, drinking the whisky
turning on the ignition. I see him

packing the boxes, his life into boxes
why did he need them? was there a chance
he'd change his mind? his battered old clothes?
 his diary in that tiny writing
all those lists of things to do, IOU's ?

it was on our block, our retreat, our happy place
our bit of bush, wombats and stringy-barks
he loved the fire, had it lit early morning
brought me my tea while he cooked the eggs
did he choose it on purpose, like choosing the date?
no, all he could possibly plan was escape

having been banished, the image creeps in
the car, the boxes, the body
deep in the bush, our bush
I knew where he'd be by the postmark
 yes of course they arrived too late
we were warned not to 'view' him

carbon monoxide makes a terrible mess
so my picture is more benign:
his head slumped over the wheel
the mop of black curls I loved
in the car with the boxes

Like Strangers

Meredith S. Grant

We're standing beside one another like two strangers in a crowd. To look at him, he doesn't look sick, as for me, I pretend not to be broken. I'm forced to explain to the emergency triage nurse why we're here and she's careful not to stare at my son for too long before asking us to take a seat amongst the crowded room.

We're surrounded with unwanted noise, noise I know won't be helping his fragile mind, his thoughts; his mood. He's fidgety, pulling at those loose threads hanging from the bandage that's covering fresh wounds on his forearm. It's hard to imagine anyone slicing a razor across their flesh, leaving precision cuts that come from one frantic moment of mind numbing absence, and I'm afraid, afraid where this might end.

I want to gently touch him, to pull him close so he can feel my warmth but instinct stops me from doing lots of things lately. I expect tears, but instead strength has joined me, how dare it, how dare I feel strength at a time like this.

He asks me how much longer we need to wait and I don't know. The kid opposite us is staring at my son's bandages and I'm forced to smile his way. I can feel the tension building and I'm worried my boy will get up and walk out those doors telling us all to get fucked, and who could blame him. I don't think much of this thing called depression or how it's invaded my son's life. Meds are not working, psychiatrists and psychologists have no answers. I despise its ability to cripple him and to tear us apart. I hate its punishing capacity to come and go as it pleases.

Finally we're led into a small impersonal room. She tells us her name but neither of us hear nor care what it was. She's not sympathetic nor empathic, instead she looks tired but so are we. My boy has no remorse or hesitation in answering her questions, he's angry, rude and it's unlike him. He responds in detail, with conviction, taking us all by surprise and suddenly this all becomes real. He has an agenda, a plan unlike any you could imagine. Words like 'hang' and 'rope' and 'home' ring in my ears, they're deafening, crushing. Those words leave us momentarily speechless as she witnesses the heaviness of grief envelope my heart, leaving me stiff and cold from the sheer veracity of it all.

I want to scream out loud, but instead I silently beg him to stop with all this honesty. I'll do whatever it takes to protect him, I don't know how, but I say I will, I'll say whatever I have to just to keep him.

Our souls sit apart like two empty milk bottles, drained and robbed of any goodness. We are so removed, so out of sync, so out of touch. When did we become such enemies without reason, without resolution, without regret?

Four Portmeirion Plates

Jane Rafe

For my Mother

Cyclamen, Hyacinth, Crocus, Aquilegia,
Four Portmeirion plates
Arranged on the draining board.
I found them yesterday at a market,
Quite unexpected amongst the bric-a-brac.
Your granddaughter said: 'Buy them! She knows
You like them; she'll be glad you spent her gift
On something nice.'

Then this morning, catching sight of them
(Lined up one behind the other in the rack)
A sharp sense of home flew in,
The air was charged with
A sadness almost comforting, a feeling
That home can be here in this place
I have resided these twenty-odd years.

And I thought of you,
The loss of not having you here
In our lives; of you not seeing
Your granddaughter grow,
Sharing her stories, hearing her laugh;
And I remembered as a child
Drinking tea from your Portmeirion cups,
You still have them, still in use,
And later, on a visit, standing in the shop with you
Wishing we could buy more.

Cyclamen, Hyacinth, Crocus, Aquilegia;
I breakfast on the world's waking side
As you drink night-time cocoa on the other—
Four Portmeirion plates,
Bringing me home.

Well-Insulated

Bronwyn Blaiklock

It's the conversations with the fridge
that tell me we've crossed the line.

Its hum is a cicada monotone
tuned to your voice
an early-warning system

that brings back childhood
in the 70s, the buzz of
the old man's Kelvinator

squatting in the corner of his shed
belly full of shiny blue cans.
A lifetime of lemonade.

Then a familiar rattle sets in
tells me: sit. wait it out.

Your heat-blind words cut through
land *thud thud thud* beside me
the same arc as the last time

a chuckle from the
whitegoods is my entry.
I fall in, wedge

into the conversation
a shelf of possibilities
icy cold, well-insulated.

Your words are rattled
by the new trajectory.

Big Grief

Connie Easterbrook

You don't really 'get' grief, until it happens to you. Then you became an unwilling and unsuspecting member of the 'grief club'. I'm talking about the kind of grief that takes over you like a dumper at the beach and spits you out the other side—dazed, confused, wild and messy.

I have lost three people I loved. It started with a phone call. Each time. A damned phone call. Phone calls that converted my life from BC into AD—three times. I had a message to call my mother as soon as possible. I rang, expecting the ordinary. I hung up, forever changed. I shouted, I screamed—this could not be real. I could not make sense of the words I was hearing.

'Danny is dead, he has taken his own life.' How could this be happening? To my brother? My happy, funny, gorgeous brother? To my ordinary, everyday kind of family. It was intense, bizarre and shocking. Strange physical sensations, emotional turmoil, mental and spiritual confusion. And an unrelenting need to know why? Why? To try and make sense of the insensible. The world didn't make sense anymore.

Christmas Day, 10 years later. A phone call. Another phone call.

'Your mother has had a stroke. Come to the hospital as soon as you can.'

A stroke—a massive bleed in her brain which ended in her death the next day. Dazed, shocked, sick, this can't be happening—today, why today?

Two years later. I check my phone, three missed calls from my husband. I call, I want to know if our daughter has made it home from university ok. I worried about her on the roads. My husband's voice sounded very strange. I forced him to tell me what was going on. The world goes black, my ears are ringing, I can hear my voice shouting, but unsure where the sound is coming from. A horrible weight pushes down on me. I am numb. I am thinking nothing, but I have a million scattered thoughts. I cannot walk. I see my family. The doctor is speaking. I cannot hear. I see my daughter, lying so still and silent, lying where she should not be.

It is nearly eight years since the car accident that took her life. It is the hardest loss of all. I have a Simone shaped hole inside of me. My daughter was an amazing paradox—passionate but infuriating, enthusiastic but overwhelming, unique and quirky but frustrating and difficult. And this is what makes my grief so painful, my belief that I never got our relationship right. I never felt like I was a 'good enough' mother. I feel cheated because I never got the chance to fix it, to be the mother I wanted to be, to complete our journey, and to say a final

'I'm sorry.'

Augustus Street

Kit Kelen

I see you there on the worn terrace stairs, doing the daily junkie impression. Or the fingerprick test to see where you're at. It's all new to me, but it's your life. Not obvious where the sunlight is from but something is cooking, the rocket ship fridge accompanies. All lean to the radio. Early days of the Hawke and Keating show and Enmore is our territory. Leaf against concrete—like a war starting then. We were on a kind of frontier. There was an anarchist bookshop.

You were upstairs. Downstairs, I was a kind of doorkeeper—foam bed on milkcrates. Italian parsley wild in the garden. Always tabouleh time. Garage full of communist stuff, and motoguzzi—which seemed to me—as an unbeliever—something like a Zenonian victory of the parts over the whole. The more work you did the less distance the machine would go.

I was in the party and you were a sometime fellow travelling. Haze of smoke we stood in. You—fighting fit, off cycling in places I might have hitchhiked once but now I was employed.

One night the dope cookies vanished and afternoon of the next day Mr ManyHours-Sleep who'd needed the sugar, came stumbling down the bleary stairs with accusation cum revelation—'it was the cookies—the cookies!'

We were going to free Nelson Mandela—I think we did. I was always grand in narrative. You taught that life was tinkering, that soup could be made out of a pumpkin without recourse to a bamix.

Even then you were the bloke with the short straw. Fate fixed you more tangibly. But we sought contradictions together, made ironies for art.

Under the pain and the bleary ending—Loftus Davros Elucidator, mastermind of an Underground, Smackaboy of Murchie girl childhoods, wry smile and wise counsel, friend. Things fall apart. You did—a kind of showing the way no one chooses.

If there's a heaven… if there's an after… if is the best we can honestly say (blessed those for whom belief is culture)…Odds infinitesimal, still that's the virtue of a universe as good as infinite—then why should not the soul be possible? The breath of a dream must rest somewhere.

How can anything be lost?

So I have a place in mind where you are able-bodied, alert, astute; where rapturous Christians linger in hells they've cooked up. But you have Billy Bragg and bicycles, Paul Kelly. You're taking it all one act at a time. Looking down from the top of the stairs, steady into steps of a parodic dance Elvis Costello croons to. Yours is a sure footed cynicism for arsehole authority.

You bear witness, bear with us the world that's passing. The struggle came to you, till you lived with the everyday tussle to be.

And so I say these last words left, however little they may mean—'go well, Dave, go well'.

Response To Murder

Mary Beneforti

You'll never forget
The phone call at work
The policeman's knock late at night
The way your mother buckled in your arms
As you bore the unspeakable news
Your brother lying in his coffin
His face swaddled in bandages
Because they wouldn't let you look at him
Because of what had been done to him
You'll never forget
Stroking his cold hands
Patting his swathed forehead
Or the stains that persisted on the walls of his house
Even though they'd been cleaned
Silent witnesses now
You'll never forget
Carrying his ashes home on the plane
Something darkly comedic about sending him
Through the x ray machine
He would have thought it funny
But nothing funny about your Dad's collapse and
Descent into dementia and your mother's
Growing disconnectedness as she regards him
Like a relative once removed not her
Husband of over 60 years
Her memories torpedoed by shock and grief
While you . . . you have let yourself go
Yet you are detained
Your emotions seethe behind
Razor wire
And you are so sad.

Two Weeks

Verity Borthwick

She grieves once a month. It's a fairly set timetable. It always comes after two weeks, the hope grows a little each day, though she wishes it wouldn't, tries to stop it, clamp it down putting hands over it. But it always wells up in the end, up between her fingers like tiny, silver bubbles. It's buoyant like that.

It's this hope that's the problem. Without it the whole thing would be easier. And it's started to feel false now anyhow, like a used car salesman trying to sell you a rusted bomb with crappy mileage, all toothy grins and waving arms.

They all tell her not to give it up, to give up that hope, as though if she ceases to believe, even for an instant, it will be over—Santa Claus was Uncle Frank in a red suit with a pillow shoved down the front—she will ruin the magic. And perhaps the magic is important, and it is her fault, and she's ruined it now because she can't believe.

On the day she bleeds again she will cry so hard she might turn inside out. Then she'll wash her face and call the nurses. Start again. A new month. She will swipe in at reception, you have an access card; they know you will be back and back and back.

She lives her life in nines. Counting forward, a calendar in her head to imagine star signs and seasons, plans for an escape from this limbo. She is not alone in this, she sits in the morning with a roomful of women who live these silent lives of nines. They move through their worlds like wraiths, through workplaces and birthday parties and Christmas, saying 'someday' when asked if they want. And they will be asked again and again. They are of a certain age you see.

She will hold out her arm to wait for the needle sting, the warm flow of blood, wish for the nurse with the purple shoes who never makes it hurt. She will mix medicines from beautiful bottles—ampules, a lovely word which she must break. She'll lift her shirt and plunge needles of icy liquid into soft flesh, wriggle toes for distraction. She'll spread her legs in front of strangers and admit machines into her body. She'll look up at the ultrasound screen, at the black hole inside her that is an egg and try to believe that such a dark nothing could ever be a child.

And this time she definitely won't hope, knows she can't do it again, knows to shut the door in its face, to think of other things. But it always finds a way in—two weeks is a long time after all—a window she forgot to lock, a door that blows open in the wind, and it will pool, warm in her belly until she is sure, so sure that it has finally worked.

She thinks that every time.

Getting To Know Grief

Carolyn Wilkinson

Grief has been hanging around all of my life. He introduced himself in childhood pets who came and went, and began hovering in my teens when, with a whiff of pipe smoke, my grandfather died. In the year when I failed University we all went to give blood in March and Jeanette was diagnosed with leukaemia. When she succumbed in October Grief swept me into the tutorial of dying young. Next He burst through the door with Mum and Geoff to tell me that Dad had not woken up one morning. This time Grief got physical, binding and setting me aside from everyone I knew as I tried and failed to make sense of what had happened. I remember a night out when no one knew what to say so they didn't say an thing at all, and I found that Grief is no form of company.

He came back when I started bleeding out my first pregnancy, and got a little nasty when the registrar was pregnant herself. He couldn't even show me what I had lost—now we know but this was 25 years ago. It happened again with my third pregnancy but now Grief was familiar so it was not so bad—we had adjusted to each other somewhat. Then our beloved Marna died, and I met Him halfway staying with her and taking her great-grand-children to say goodbye. Grief is a little kinder when it's all as expected, and you can lay out the ground rules together.

Years later and He came back in the door as my husband walked out taking our marriage with him. He looked different clothed as He was this time in embarrassment and regret as well. He hung around as the court case dragged on, and poked a hole in my heart each time I had to turn up. I discovered journaling so we talked, and I realised He had much to share with me. Grief though was threatening to run my life and eventually I got up the courage for a show down one weekend up the coast, and asked Him to leave. And He did.

I realised He wasn't done when we were told that my husband of not even a year had metastatic melanoma. Everyone kept trying to push Him away in the four months he had left but I alone knew He was staying. The day Gary died Grief broke my heart into a thousand pieces and I reluctant-ly agreed to travel the road of mourning with Him. Grief is slowly showing Himself to actually be Suffering, and not just mine but ours. Every one of us. And there are glimpses, if I will see them, of Love. I know Him today in my Mum as she struggles to the end of her life, and we say goodbye forever each time I see her. Sometimes you can sort it out with Grief on your own terms. And perhaps even be Friends.

Nourishing The Spirit

Rachael Mead

The first law of thermodynamics

It was a day like lost love, the earth
holding puddles of sky as keepsakes.
Footsteps muffled to murmurs,
I walked to the bridge, its stone legs
astride a tombstone of cold shadow.

At the gate, the dogs flushed out a white sedan,
wheels failing at the mechanics of friction.
The passenger wound down her window.
We're not littering. Our son died here. It's for him.
Her tight smile held back mouthfuls of grief.
We thought the foxes would take care of it.

Laid out on a bright spread of newspaper
was the offering, a picnic memorial
for the boy and the man, both lost
at the end of this midwinter track.
The cheese sandwich sliced just so,
a sweet sultana log, loss still brewing
in the milky coffee, the half-smoked
rollie propped on a stone, smoke
curling into the air like incense.

I stood before the fleeting altar,
the equation describing the miracle
that energy is never lost
a cold comfort when those left
can't see their son in the swivel of stars,
hear his voice in the rush of the creek.
With nothing more to offer than silence
I left it there for physics and the foxes
to do their dark and thankless work.

Metal Cries

Annie Barrett

I drive along the bay into suburbs I once knew and pass a sad, forgotten place. I park and walk settling into the reverent ambiance, looking for letters and numbers. It is thirty four years since I stepped on this grass. Finally I find Lawn D, Row F of the Cemetery.

The numbers are not logical. I wander back and forth looking down, counting, confused and then there in front of me he lies, decayed bones now. My tears surprise me.

I place a small white rose beside the plaque submerged in healthy grass, and wonder if the white rose bush his mother gave me is still flowering in the garden of the home where we last made love.

I remember those photos that rested for years on bookcases. My first lover, blue-eyed and tall, with a mullet haircut, flared jeans and athletic body laughed, as he bent over a cricket bat. In another he stood shirtless, handsome, happy, that first summer up in the Victorian high country. Now snatches of memory remain,my heart is soft.

I listen to the swish of tyres on the wet road outside the wire fence and remember his funeral day. I thought his grave was on a slight hill, but it is flat. Then the cemetery seemed empty, now there seems to be no room for another body. It felt desolate, forlorn. Today it is strangely peaceful.

Visitors wander quietly, some with bunches of flowers. I look up and we smile gently as we pass. It is a hello-goodbye place.

Soon after visiting his grave I drive southeast towards Wilson's Promontory National Park. There is no white roadside cross with flowers. It was a time before those memorials appeared and became a reminder to slow down, a reminder to love. Which two trees did he hit with the cry of screeching metal?

At his December funeral the priest to my horror said he was a Christmas Present for Jesus! A few weeks later his friends and I gathered at the Prom. We drank warm moselle flagon wine. I swallowed my sorrow, and numbed my longing for his strong arms around me, for his love.

Now I clamber over huge granite boulders. I don't remember this rugged beauty, I only remember the lonely nights with friends and faint light layered through bushy trees.

A ferocious sound plays through the treetops and below it brings gusts of grit. A eucalypt grimaces in the wind. Leaves lift and bow and expose their soft grey undersides, then right themselves before the next blast.

The southerly gale at the Prom is blowing questions back into me and through me. I knew all those years ago that I couldn't live with those questions, I let them and my lingering guilt go. Now they are like ripples, not Victorian back-beach waves full of kelp ready to wrap around my body and drown me. Just ripples, I don't mind their presence. I feel held in this granite place.

The Tilted House

Simeon Kronenberg

She lived at a slight angle to the universe,
      and laughed, delighted at the world.

But she was odd, like a deer in a tree,
      and when illness came, her life swayed

away from her—she lurched, forced to learn
      again how to walk, talk and shit.

Friends saw the helpless effort to stay
      recognisable at least, despite the sudden

mugging in her head as the tumour beat her up.
      And, finally, she couldn't remember directions

home, she cried (we thought she was stoned
      or drunk, she hoped she was).

The tumour galloped and they took it out
      and after, she staggered on for a bit—

like a new colt, lopsided.
      And, near the end, tut-tutting, her mother

came for her and fussed. After, in Winchester,
      her father muttered into his paper

waiting to be fed and she sat, blurred
      for days, drifting in a too-warm room,

staring at her mother's English garden.
      She missed her white-limbed citreodora

and acacia and kangaroo paw and banksia
      and hosing down her windows in the palpable

heat on the sloped street in Clifton Hill,
      her tilted house, wide, weatherboard, her own.

The Thief

Taylor Jane

I remember the first time I notice the thief take something from you. You are making your morning coffee, I am busy about the kitchen getting breakfast, our usual morning routine. It is then that I see that the thief has entered your life. Someone unfamiliar to you wouldn't notice the subtle change in the mundane, the way that you are slow to get the mug from the cupboard, the way you rigidly pour the coffee from the percolator. The struggle with the sugar jar, your confidence shaken when pouring the milk. It is this that makes me notice.

The thief creeps in slowly at first, taking things so gradually, it is barely detectable. Stealing small things at a time, then almost appearing to be halting, leaving the illusion that nothing else would be taken. I almost convince myself that he is not real. But the thief has his grasp on you, and he won't let you go.

Just when you have forgotten his presence, the thief punctuates the mundane with force. I am to drive you home. We get in the car, you struggle with the seat belt, you cannot do it. I agonise, unsure what to do. Whether to sit here in silence and let you keep trying, pretending it is not happening, or to lean over quickly and do it for you, admitting you can no longer do this simple task.

All of a sudden he gains momentum, as if going on a raid, and soon the loss would be so great it would take my breath away, my eyes flooding with tears when you are not looking.

Many times you rise above the thief, defy him, allowing him no victory. You walk me down the aisle. The father of the bride speech, your voice shaking and quiet, but despite that it is a moment you do not allow him to steal. At times you are able to take things back from the thief. Despite the odds you recognise my son as your grandson. It is on reflection on these moments, that I know that though he may try, the thief can never take all of you. There is part of you that it is impossible for him to touch. You will always continue on, despite whatever he takes.

Over time the thief steals more and more from you, sometimes stealing slowly, sometimes rapidly, but always with the knowledge that there is nothing we can do to lock him out.

Early in the morning, Easter morning, the thief makes his final strike. There is no more he can take, you are gone. Gone.

The Coat

Julie Manning

For a man predisposed to all things
lacking substance, my father's special gift, once a year,
was nylon jackets—
a stiff outer shell with fake fur hood,
the lining quilted and stitched with flying geese.
We fought over leaf green and carmine.

How this frugal man could rifle
through catalogues, alone in his office, his outline a shadow
thrown from a desk lamp, selecting patterns
and button styles from a Hong Kong pamphlet,
mystified me.

At school events, an empty chair had dark meaning
He gave us gifts instead, things procured
from the station wagon displays of travelling salesmen;
a child's manicure set, boxed cosmetics, our jackets—
whatever a man buried in management could bring
to bridge two worlds.

In our car coats we weren't poor, or from a cold, uncultured house
the silk lining with the bone toggle-buttons
kept us from self-admonishment.

At the rugby I stood beside him, our hands in pockets,
coloured coats marking us out
as some species of exotic visitor
blown from the sidelines of a city, the sharp sky
reflected in the ice of wheel-ruts.

Cars, bonnet-first, ringed the country oval.
My father, in heavy concentration, would shout periodically,
the late winter sun striking sparks from his lions club badge,
his woolen fleck drawn tight to his throat.

It was hard to tell the high call of a bird
from the full time whistle dying out in the wind,
but I did not know then who my father was
beyond the man beside me,
his scarf like a collar some animals wear in winter.

Between

Jenny Pollak

Today I can grieve. Slung like an eye
between two centuries.
Years like poultices.

I think of shadows as indulgences
we tried not to get lost in.
Better to follow the slant of a transitory light.

Your smile when it came was so deep
your head fell back when you laughed.
All the shadows were behind you.

Lullaby I Never Wished to Sing

Audrey M. Molloy

After Brahms

She's excited, has her kids
And her husband beside her
Gel is glossy on her belly
In the screen's silvery light

Back at home, on their fridge
A small grainy photo
Taken only last week
Of a jelly bean mid-kick

I ask kindly that he leaves
Takes the children outside
She's still smiling, has no notion
Hasn't seen what I have seen

I do not utter *dead*
Just *No sign of a heart beat*
The heat map shows no colour
Like her face above the sheet

She is staring at the baby
She will never get to hold
Then they go home together
Mother and dead child

Though she floats in her womb
She is all on her own
In her watery tomb
No one even knew she'd gone

The Very In-Between

Hannah van Didden

My name is Lara Strong and my husband is dead.

Three months after it happened, to the day, I meet the men who will level our house. Their wrecking ball's parked out front when I get there.

'Sorry I'm late,' I say to the two nuggety blokes who greet me at the door. It's like we're in uniform: my camisole is the same blue as their singlets, but I doubt their pants are from Saba.

'No problem, darlin',' the first man says. 'Take yer time.'

The way he licks his lips in his survey of the place disturbs me.

The other guy is quieter. 'Many memories here?'

My key finds the lock and I lower my gaze. His hand on my shoulder breaks me from whatever it is that's come over me.

'I'm okay,' I say to his boots, because I am.

I would have booked it to come down the day after the funeral if I could have. I had already moved into mum's, put the big-ticket items into storage, let his family pick at his possessions. Who would have thought that one could collect so many real estate magnets?

'Take some time to think it over,' mum had said.

'How long?' I asked.

She suggested a year. Three months was all I could manage.

Now guy number two tells me to take some time, to say goodbye.

I nod but I feel like this is an expectation thrust upon me. This is unnecessary sentiment. I just want it to be done.

Still, I walk from room to room, fabricating hope from the familiarity like my husband is somehow caught in between this world and the next. I'm waiting for him to jump at me from behind a door, to laugh over his brilliant *gotcha*. He doesn't.

The house is blank without him and our things. I run fingers through dusty surfaces, bid farewell to the bedroom and bathroom and lime-green-and-orange kitchen that somehow stayed my favourite room.

The kitchen. Where he made our meals. Where he taught me how to clean grout with a diamond-edged piece of plastic. Where I had justified the presence of both a dishwasher and a dryer in the house. Where I told him about our baby.

From here, he would produce miraculous treats when the emotion demanded. Miraculous, I say, because I only discovered his chocolate hidey-hole on the day he passed, when I attacked the kitchen cabinets with his crowbar and my bare hands. Looking for the stupid, stupid cat!

Then I see the grout amid two splash-back tiles, yellowed but brighter than the grout around it, with the small hole in the middle he'd blushed over because his demonstration had been too vigorous. This is it—the first place he'd shown me to use the grout cleaner, the very in-between.

I offer to pay for petrol and the time I've wasted. Guy number one is all under-breath expletives and over head hand gestures. Guy number two just presses back on my hand.

The Visit

Jill Slack

Her whole past, she tells me,
boils down to a series of razorbacks;
she survives by riding the brakes
hand on horn and heart in mouth.
She rubs a scar on her shin,
lasting legacy of a rabid dog bite
when she was an unhappy bride
years before in Singapore.

We stir sugar into our tea
in her tiny dark kitchen, the stove winks red-eyed,
and eat wafer-thin slices of black fruitcake—
her grandmother's recipe from her Atherton years.
Her parents suicided on her ninth birthday—
but she doesn't quite believe it:
more like he killed her then shot himself.

Right now she's up against
the nailed-down convictions that old age
is the wrong side of the precipice
You'd already crossed the Rubicon at fifty,
all but useless, like a single bar of signal—
she flutters a derisive hand at my iPhone,
proud of her grasp of this new nonsense.

The inevitability of nursing home appals her.
Such bad karma for oldies
(her quavering voice suddenly biblical),
so wrong of children to insist.
Her grandmother lay down and died
in her own bed, in her own house at age ninety-five.

It's what she will have for herself;
at her own pace, in her own time
and in the very bed where
her treacherous children were conceived,
where her dour spouse breathed his last.
She looks me full in the face
would serve them right, wouldn't it?

Villanelle For My Mother

Rory K. Hudson

I heard my mother's fingers fall
on the piano's keys with distant sound:
first slow, then seldom—lastly, not at all.

As destiny began to call
from some far-off unnoticed ground,
I heard my mother's fingers fall

and wrap her memories in a shawl
to warm her as she moved around,
first slow, then seldom—lastly, not at all.

The world so wide, and she so small—
yet in the solitude I found
I heard my mother's fingers fall

to play some notes she could recall
from former days that might rebound
first slow, then seldom—lastly, not at all.

I've seen the grasses growing tall
beside my mother's marbled mound;
and I have heard her fingers fall
first slow, then seldom—lastly, not at all.

Soup

Janet Haigh

The water swelled around his calves, a cool grasping at his skin, and he cupped it to press the heat from his eyes. Emily would visit this afternoon.

Gripping another bundle of cress, he pulled it, roots and all, from the sandy bottom of the spring, and stepped out to push his way through the ferns and blackberries at the end of the garden.

Back in the kitchen, he stamped cold feet on the lino. He added the peppery leaves to the stock; then fresh peas; a sprinkle of nutmeg. Reaching into the drawer for a spoon, he snatched his hand back, heart jerking, recoiling from the blue enamel of Addie's favourite cutlery as he would from a spider.

He stumbled over her presence in all the usual places—kitchen, garden, bedroom—all the inevitable, hollow spaces that made up a home. With her physically gone, he imagined her into being more animated than she'd been perhaps, more vocal. Happier, he thought guiltily. All the best bits magnified by absence, their regular, dull sniping shaded out.

Placing one earthenware bowl on her dusty side table, he set the enamel spoon beside it. An offering of sorts. From the corner of his eye, he saw the steam rise and coil, a hint of movement to trick his mind—while it still gave off heat, he could pretend that she'd just stepped out to grab her book, maybe answer the phone.

He lifted the soup to his mouth. The taste had him gagging on the sudden memory of her quick hands at work, stripping peas, in the garden. The once comforting liquid stuck like a bone in his throat but, determined, he swallowed the heat down and brushed sweat from his upper lip with the back of a hand. The meal left an aftertaste of shared summer evenings; the wordless criticism of sizzled pot plants, the crack of thunder at dinnertime signalling and heavy rain.

Lifting his chin to face her photograph, he frowned. Addie glared darkly from behind the frame, challenging him. She looked disappointed.

'Hush, hush.' He shook his head, murmuring to himself, cradling the quickly cooling bowl. The sludgy, chlorophyll-coloured liquid reminded him of pond water. She always did it better, but how in the hell did she get it so smooth? A mystery.

Down the hallway, the doorbell rang. It was early. Wasn't it? As he opened the screen-door, he could feel his face smiling too brightly.

'Come in, come in.'

'Oh Dad.' Emily looked at him, distraught and exasperated, raising a hand to shield her eyes from the weight of his care.

Following her gaze, he looked down at the saturated cuffs of his trousers, the blackberry shards in his palms and the clods of earth trailed across the carpet. He bit his lip, seeing Addie in every anxious, caring line of his daughter's face.

He smiled, took her hand. 'Come in. I made soup.'

Vigil

Ann M Poore

(An understated dignity
Shrouded in silence
And quiet reflection).

Blood pools to the lowest point,
Elbows and heels mottled purple,
Sharp contrast the sallowing skin.

The air bed breathes in and out,
Mocking semblance of breath
To confuse the watcher.

And endings mirror beginnings,
As wrapped and swaddled,
The lying-in begin.

Autumn, A Mother's Grief

Mark Miller

It always begins with smells—

the vaporised frost at dawn
infused with mulched leaves of the garden

the scent of eucalyptus
under pungent drops of an afternoon squall

the chimney-smoke thick with pine,
and heavy with evening's dew—

it always begins with smells—
the mustiness of a shut room

the staleness of potpourri in the upper
corner of the dresser drawer

the photo album clumsily disturbed,
the images evoking

the taffeta-smell of the christening gown,
the milk-dribble of the infant in a woman's arms

the priest's incense and tobacco-steeped garments,
the earthiness of the raw clay mound

on the cemetery's bitten lawn.

The Teacher's Daughter

Laura Greaves

It had been a bad year for uncomfortable conversations. First there was the boy with leukemia. Terribly sad, but not unexpected. And a charity had sent him to Hawaii to bodyboard at Pipeline, remember? So that was something.

Then there was the year twelve boy found hanged. An accident, they told you at assembly. Adamant. But you knew better. You all knew better.

When the girl was run over, the grown-ups had a meeting and decided: moving swiftly on was best. *They're just kids*. It wouldn't do to dwell. Nothing to see here.

You were late to drama class. When you rushed in the atmosphere was heavy. *What happened?* A girl died. A teacher's daughter. Hit on the highway yesterday. Now, back to Stanislavsky.

You put your hand to your cheek, sure you'd been slapped. This news was violent. The teacher's daughter was your friend. It took an hour to force down a breath You kept picturing your bare feet propped up on the dashboard of your father's car yesterday. While he drove you home from a party, the teacher's daughter died in an ambulance.

You wore your tear-stained face in the corridor. A grown-up told you to put it away in your locker. *Come on, that's enough for today.* People stared. *She knew the dead girl.* They looked away then. Best not to make a fuss. Nothing to see here.

Mum was shocked. *Was she the girl who was here last week?* No. That was another friend whose name sounds similar. Oh. Mum's relief was a living thing. She couldn't quite recall the teacher's daughter and that made it so much better for her. She could get on with making dinner. Nothing to see here.

Dad called. *When I was your age, I had a friend who died.* How did you bear it, Dad? How did you live? *You move on. You're just kids. Life continues.* Nothing to see here.

What you didn't do was talk about it. About her. Didn't talk about how she loved to dance and knew all the songs from The Lion King by heart. *Best not to make a fuss.* Didn't think about the sugary scent of her Body Shop perfume. *It doesn't do to dwell.* Tried to forget the time she sobbed *you wouldn't care if I died* in front of the cool girls who tormented her. Refused to remind yourself how they laughed and agreed. *Moving swiftly on is best. Nothing to see here.*

Life did go on. They taught you Maths and Science. Grief was not on the curriculum. They didn't teach you how to make sense of it. So you tried to figure it out. You stumbled slowly forward. They couldn't have known how the teacher's daughter would haunt you. They couldn't have known what a teacher she would be.

The Crumbling Cliff

Julia Maciver

It takes a minute to remember in the mornings. Mum's dead. The constant of my life is gone and I'm drifting. I'll never be able to ask her advice, see her smile, eat her roast chicken, ever again.

Every day I walk along a crumbling cliff. Darkness tugs at me, inviting me to step over the edge, to embrace the numbness and join her in oblivion. It's tempting, but every time I'm about to give in life drags me back. There's simply too much to do, kids to organise, lunches to pack, clothes to wash and that's all before I leave for work. I don't have time to deal with the writhing tangle of emotions in my belly right now, so I push it down and plaster a smile on my face.

Keep walking along the cliff edge. Don't look down.

Now and then I stumble and I'm over the edge, dangling in the darkness. There's no rhyme or reason: the smell of fresh baked bread, a snippet of song, the softness of a merino scarf, it seems like anything can send me over that cliff. I hang there dazed, shackled by peoples' demands until yet another need wraps around me, pulling me up, dragging me back from despair.

Each day more ropes wrap around me, tugging me further away from the cliff's edge. The ground gets more solid under my feet. Some days I forget that the cliff is even there. The demands of my life keep me busy and days go past when I don't think of her at all. Then the guilt crashes down. How could I ever forget her? How can I not care that she is gone? What kind of a daughter am I? Everything collapses and I'm back hanging over the darkness, waiting for the ropes to pull me back up.

Life goes on until one day I burst into tears trying to convince my daughter to eat her carrots, so she will see better in the dark. That's exactly how mum got me to eat carrots, at least until I broke my wrist falling down the stairs in the dark after eating a bag of them. Charlotte gapes at me as my sobs turn into laughter. Mum's not really gone. As long as I remember all the things she taught me then she is still with me. Her strength, her wisdom are a part of me. If I listen closely I can still hear her voice and the voices of the others who've gone ahead. I don't need her beside me to ask her advice; I know what she would have said.

Now when I think of Mum we're walking along a beach at the bottom of the cliff. It wasn't the chasm I thought it was, just a sea cliff as the sun rises.

Grieving

Annette Allen

His voice, a thin
tenor I hear

singing, a presence
near my elbow,

times past seep
their nostalgia into

the present, the notes
weeping in acquiescence,

welling like the salt
in my eyes, the memories

like the drooping of these
white rose buds in their vase,

still beautiful, brilliant
but sad, their sadness bell-
shaped . . .

reminding me of the diagnosis
that quickly drained life
from him

and of the bell
that tolled for him, on
a yesterday not long gone.

Adrift

Holly Bruce

The torpedo hit as I woke. Full force—still—after all these months. I circle directionless struggling to stay afloat; existing in a world weighted in memory, imagination, and longing.

It takes the entire morning to orient myself. I move through the house anchoring my body on items of furniture to steady the rush and wash in my head. The house ticks and sighs, a long suffering witness to my solo act.

Wal, though he is long gone, is everywhere. He is an echo in the bathroom, where he whistles to his reflection in wavering Vivaldi. He is a rattle in the kitchen, measuring tea with a pharmacist's precision. The hymn of my husband: I have been attuned to his soundtrack for sixty-five years.

I pitch myself onward down the hallway, where I am met by Wal's beloved Russian Blue. Reggie is also in search of what he cannot find. He rubs his rack of ribs against my ankle; bone on bone. I see his nine lives are almost up: the inflexible gait, a dimming of eyes, his ragged soprano.

By midday my balance is restored to a functional level. The doctor tells me there is no physical reason for my loss of equilibrium. Wal's death has knocked me off my feet. Time heals, he hastens to add. At eighty-eight, time is a luxury I have little of. My social straight-jacket deters me from stating the obvious.

Bills litter the hall table, autumn leaves strewn by a wounding westerly. I gather them into my handbag, feed Reggie, and begin the laborious process of readying myself for a trip to the shops.

At the post office the queue snakes forward; a slow painful crawl. I reach the counter and hand over my documents. Questions are fired, the answers unknown. It was Wal who dealt with these matters of finance. Without him life has no currency.

The assistant goes about her processing, an efficient robot.

'Cash or card' she asks, without raising her eyes from the terminal. I hand her the fifties and watch, mesmerised, as she flicks through them.

I ache to tear free of my polite façade, to hurl my jagged grief—like a bomb—into the space between us, but the assistant gazes beyond me and hands me the receipts: my time is up.

Swirling litter dances past the bus stop. I sit and wait.

The bus jolts and shudders through side streets. I labour through land-scape that is both familiar and foreign. All that Wal no longer sees blurs and fades.

Reggie is waiting when I arrive at the house. I lift him to my shoulder, no easy feat. He bleats into my neck, inconsolable.

The pin on my compass has been pulled. True north lost, a land beyond reach.

I totter to the sunroom, dark now. A foreign country, all tools of navigation gone. I sink to the life raft of Wal's armchair and cling to Reggie.

Dichotomy

Ingrid Coote

There's a movie playing in my head. It's been running since you died, every hour of every day for the past five years. The memories of our life together are set on a permanent loop somewhere in the back of my brain. In the beginning, the show reel was all consuming and painful. Now was just numbness, the future was no more than an hour away.

I had enough presence of mind back then to warn everyone that I couldn't plan beyond the current day. Being able to think a day ahead eventually became two, then a week, and now, five years on, about a month. Maybe it will never be more than that.

I feel like two completely different versions of myself. There's the 'old me' who everyone sees; seemingly still the same person, so much so that perhaps people even forget what's happened. The other, 'new me', is still constantly re-living our movie. Sometimes it's sad, sometimes romantic, occasionally it's a witty comedy. The only present you and I have is in my head—and it's so very precious.

I'm still coming to terms with the contradictions of this new life. How is it possible for me to be functional in the every-day world when the bigger picture is so broken? Mother, breadwinner, property owner, daughter, friend, employee. There's not much time and space for me as the grieving wife. Perhaps this is why our movie plays subconsciously, giving me a chance to fit you in.

I would never have believed I could find the strength to tell you it was okay to go, and then pick myself up and keep living. I used to wish our places could be reversed so I didn't have to be the one to go on. Now I am grateful that I am still here; and that I have discovered I am strong enough to do this for both of us.

Life is now so very different, but some things strangely remain the same. I watch our sons start to achieve the goals we had together for them. There is joy and sadness in every milestone. I've learned to live with this contradiction. I'm there cheering at every sports game and assembly while holding back the tears. There's an unspoken understanding between all of us that you would be proud.

Our movie is now not all consuming, it just 'is'. I've made peace with the interruptions and busy-ness it brings to my thoughts. I sometimes catch myself smiling at what has just happened in my head. Those surprising, beautiful moments help me realise I am healing and give me renewed strength to face the future.

A Gift Returned

Adrian Caesar

(For K)

I'm glad it's me not either of the boys,
you said, *I'd rather be the one to die.*
Beside your intellectual life,
motherhood was a sacred task for you
I think–no accident your stairwell muse
a tapestry placed so each ascent was met
by Flora via Morris and Burne-Jones:
I am the handmaid of the earth. Just so,
domestic goddess, you scattered gifts,
maker and baker of daily feasts,
cook and cleaner and garden builder;
those last days in June how anxious you were
to pot the bright geraniums for summer
in courtyard and back patio: their bloom
outlasting you, as your boys live to mourn
your early passing, though surely something
of your abundance lives in them, in us,
husband, sons, father, brothers,
who bore the weight of your wicker casket
to the woodland burial at Barton Glebe—
no cremation for you—who wanted to grow
back to the mothering earth; to live
amid the birdsong and wild flowers,
scattering forth again as we sow your plot
and water our mourning seeds for you
to broider fair your lasting gown.

Things I Forgot To Ask

Laura Jean McKay

What is the flavour of company. Of country.
How does loneliness smell.
What do you eat in the afterlife.
Where are we in science, more advanced or catching up.
Who is regarded as influential.
Where are the honest few.
Why are there instruments.
Where is power, how do I hold it. Is it my fault if I feel powerless.
Have I somehow left it behind.
What makes sadness marketable.
How could you describe it someone who has never heard it whispered in
such terms.
How could you be so right and then die like that.
Were you a genius.
Did you have insight that you didn't believe in.
Was something broadcast and you heard it one day.
Was it our relationship. Did we have one.
Every time you fell into me did you really start breathing.
Why was I a solution. Does a solution go away with a problem.
What happens to a solution once it swallows a problem.
Does it become a new problem.
What do I do now.
Where do I go.
Am I an unsolved case. Will somebody find my file one day.
Read me and say, I think we have new evidence.
Will I ever become curious again. Will I ever become curious again.
I dream I am pressed against a sea wall by waves.
I wake to memory, to administrative sanity: that's right, that's correct,
you're dead.
Why is this is the day when you're not here.
How is it that you will never be here again.
Is this what life looks like on the other side of you everything swayed on
an inland wind that blows like a disease across the country.
I am strung out between neat sun bitten fence posts, empty paddocks,
chewed grass.
Why death. Why dead. Why died. Why over. Why gone. Why deceased.

Why stopped. Why passed. Why in the past.
What are the chords for this.
What is the sound of death.
How to put that to music. To words.
I tried the radio but it whined, searching for stations, settled on static.

Interventions

Lorne Johnson

I see my young neighbour
hovering outside our local cafe;

she's wrapped in her dead
husband's old Roosters jersey.

She stares blankly at silvereyes
shivering in winter birches,

zenith clouds divided by winds,
three giggly children rumbling

with a crazy curly-coated
retriever puppy named Circus.

She has turned into a sheet
of floating polar ice.

When he was flame, she
thought only of mountains.

I ask myself why I don't
take her arm, buy her a coffee.

That night, storms throttle
our town. I picture her

lying on his side
of their bed, slowly turning

his beloved Harley-Davidson
lighter between dirty fingers,

whispering the lyrics
to those AC/DC songs

he adored. I convince myself
that tomorrow, I'll walk

through pummelling rain
to reach her sinking home:

I'll throw out empty wine bottles,
wash clothes, brush her hair
and wrap her wrists.
We'll just sit by her living

room window and wait for all
the hail and sleet to melt.

Grief Delayed

Nick Carroll

When I was fifteen years old my grandfather shot dead his only son, my uncle, and then shot himself. I remember the headline in the newspaper that was delivered to our home every day, "Father, Son Found Shot."

Grandad was a small, gentle, kind man whom I loved spending time with. Uncle Jim, Mum's only sibling, was mentally and physically disabled due to having suffered incurable meningitis as a baby. He was utterly dependent on his parents. Yet despite slurred speech and spastic body movements, he was remarkably skilled: he played the piano, he was a capable fisherman, and he rode a bike. He perched me side saddle on the cross-bar and proudly paraded me around town where he was a well known identity. I was happy spending time with him.

Three years prior to that headline I stayed with Grandad and Jim while Nanna was in hospital. One night I was impelled from sleep by the loud wailing of a wounded animal. It pierced the wall between my room and Jim's. My spine froze. Grandad had just told Jim that Nanna had suddenly died from a blood clot. Nanna and Grandad had lovingly cared for Jim all his life.

That unhinged cry has never left me.

The second tragedy, which left my mother an orphan, left me with only the most prosaic memory. My siblings and I were immediately farmed out to neighbours while Mum and Dad left to deal with this brutal event one hundred and fifty miles away. When they returned they said little about what must have been a horrific experience. There was no overt grief to observe nor do I remember losing my own equilibrium. All Mum said was that Dad had been very brave and supportive when they had to confront the gruesome scene.

Fifty years later, while in the process of writing a memoir, I decided to delve into the archives. There was the headline again. The newspaper report told how Grandad had written to a family friend. The letter asked that he should take a doctor and ambulance to the residence

> *... where you will find us in Jim's bedroom on the right of the passage ... In another envelope, found wrapped in a parcel of money left in the house, was another letter. The contents indicated that the case was one of murder and suicide and that the father had been extremely worried about the future welfare of his son, who was unable to work ...*
>
> *Investigations by the police showed the son had been shot through the head and chest and that the father had died of a gunshot wound through*

the head.

A sawn–off .303 rifle was found in the room in which the two bodies were discovered lying on the one bed . . . His wife died some years ago, and he has one married daughter.

That daughter was my mother. For the first time I wept for her and for Grandad, and for Jim, and for myself.

Grandpa

Bonnie Kang

Nobody had ever shown me how to grieve. For myself or for someone else. And as a result they never saw me grieve the way people usually did: soft sobbing, crying between intermittent gasping, tortured wailing, clutching at one's chest as if their heart was about to shatter into pieces at any impending moment. But I did grieve, very privately and quietly in my nine year old soul.

Grandpa's death was not a surprise to me or anyone in the family as he had battled cancer for a while, we had become used to the slow progression of disease which was robbing him of all energy. He had been a heavy smoker for most of his life, yet, ironically it wasn't his lungs that had given way but a cancer somewhere else. I had wondered why they had him hooked to various machines in the hospital when, clearly, every time I saw him he seemed to be in more pain than in my previous visit. Why did they keep injecting him with those fluids if it didn't make him better but instead caused pain? The last time I had seen him, his legs were stiff and skinny like a tree branch. He hardly recognised me by then.

Perhaps my process of grieving had started right there and then, before his soul was freed from his body. He had been a tall and sturdy man who was not intimidated by anyone or anything, yet, in his hospital gown he shivered even with layers of sheets and blankets cocooning him. I grieved inside, never letting anyone see it because I felt like even though the battle was coming to an end, admitting to the world that I was grieving would indicate hope was lost. I wasn't alone in thinking this, I was sure, because my family had shown that same superficial resilience, going about life as usual although we all knew so well that grandpa's last chapter of life was inevitably coming to a close.

'It's strange, I don't think she's sad. She certainly doesn't look like she is,' my mum said to my dad the morning they had told me the news. I had my back to them, pretending to be asleep in my bed. I had instantly felt a pin drop inside my chest, a pang of pain and longing but I did what I did best: pretend to be okay because I was scared that the tears would allow the flood of grief to overtake me.

Many years later, my mum asked whether I was ever sad about grandpa passing away. If that pain I felt was real, yes, I had experienced sadness. Why didn't they teach us about grief at school? Since loss is universal and lifelong shouldn't it be an essential subject like English and Maths? At least then we can expect it and name it. Of course, it won't change anything. I will still hurt because I loved. Grief will remind me.

Night Piece

Stephen Smithyman

I wake in the middle of the night and look out between curtains,

open for the heat, at the sky, descending on the house at the top

of the hill across the road. Heavily pendulous, the errant constellations

tumble down the sky towards the house, brilliantly lit, from far off,

by porchlights and flickering plasma TV. Like Prometheus bringing fire

to humans, the house seems to conduct the brilliance of the night sky

to earth, but only in limited portion. The hill itself is dark, like this room

where I lie, in the house of the dying man, sweating, unable to sleep.

The Scan

Sandra Hodgen

6 December 2010

I have the scan at 3.40pm.

Our second baby's heart has stopped beating. Baby still has its egg sack. There is something about the image of that tiny embryo holding its little egg sack that wrenches my heart. They are wrong, they must be. But nothing happens on the screen. The obstetrician says he doesn't know what went wrong as a ten week old baby is too small for them to tell. He thinks it never implanted properly.

The shock is like a wall, as though the air is replaced by something semi-solid, like jelly. I hear everything they say, I nod when I should be nodding but I'm hearing through layers, slightly distorted. I'm not really here. My toddler senses something's wrong and is needier than usual, holding onto the material of my skirt as we sit in the tiny, almost window-less, room kept for these sorts of conversations. The seats are plush and comfortable to ease the awfulness of these moments. But I don't feel the cushions at all.

The smell of toddler poo fills the room. Callen needs to be changed and he has nothing to play with here. Instead we sit riveted to the seats, listening so closely to what they're telling us. As though by listening to every word being said we can change the news they're giving us. It doesn't.

Below my lungs is the rise of my belly, holding baby's body still. I am still pregnant. But I will never hold this baby in my arms. Never feed or calm baby, never see it walk or crawl.

Deep breath. Don't think.

As we leave my friend's sister walks by, going to have a scan too. She is so excited to see us here, I can see it on her face. I've not told them about my pregnancy. My friend will be calling to congratulate us. My heart hurts, and my chest aches with tears I can't let myself cry. There is a room full of happy people, waiting to see their baby for the first time, or to see how it's grown. I have to pretend it's okay. Because if I start crying I won't stop. I take rapid deep breaths. I don't even know if it was a boy or a girl. For some reason that's important. When I try to picture what my baby might be like in three years or ten, it will have no name, no identity, and no burial.

Once we're home I shut myself in our bedroom. Iain takes the rest of the day off work and looks after our little boy. My toddler comes in and brings me rusks and shoes, and cries when I do.

I fall asleep crying, my hand on my belly. When I sleep I can't feel anything. A numbness that evaporates when I wake up thinking I'm pregnant like I was yesterday and then realise with the cold gripping feeling in my middle that I'm not.

The Vase

Maree Reedman

I hadn't unpacked
everything from the washing basket
I collected from my mother's cupboard
over a year ago.
My brother spoke of a bunny plate and an egg cup
with his name on it
which was given away in a culling
of our parent's things.
Some op shop got it. Collector's items, he said.
Do you know how much they go for?
But it wasn't the money he wanted.
He was her golden child, the first-born favourite.
He reminisced about a blown green vase
he had given her as a youngster
for her birthday. It had bubbles in the base,
and a rolled-edged lip.
I know the one, I said. I liked it too, and a part of me,
a small, selfish part,
hoped it was not in the basket,
because I would have to give it to him.
I couldn't remember whether it was in the basket, but promised to
investigate.
The morning of his departure, I placed the vase on the kitchen counter.
Look, I said.
He took a step backwards, bent over and said, *Wow.*
He held it up to the light.

The Room

K. M. J. Brann

He had a house, once. A car, and a hell of a load of crap that he had accumulated over the years. Now it was replaced with a single bedroom with a bathroom attached. He didn't own that though. It was more like a guest room. He couldn't remember the last time he had left it.

From where he lay he had two views of outside the room. A window that was covered by the bushes and a corner of corridor through the door. He'd watch the nurses go by, every now and then pushing another patient along.

They'd talk about him out there. He heard parts of what they said but it was never anything good. No one spoke to him though. Even in the room, even when they were feeding him, cleaning him, they would talk to one another.

Because no one thought he could hear them. Palliative was what he heard some people say. He thought it more like running maintenance until the machine broke down. He could barely see, couldn't move, and wouldn't stop shitting himself. But his brain still worked fine, and that was the hardest part.

His kids had been by a few hours back which would be the highlight of his week. If he made it that long. They talked to him about their lives, their work and so forth. Neither of them mentioned their mother. He guessed it was hard for her as well.

She would not see the husk of him. Withered and frail. She had cared for him in the beginning but it had been a long time since she had been by. Could he blame her for that? He wondered, would he have acted differently if she had been the one who developed the cancer?

He sighed, or at least thought he had. He wanted someone to come by, didn't want to be alone there in that room. The bell was next to him but there was no strength left to push it.

It wouldn't be long now. He had held on for the kids' arrival but there was doubt he would make it for the next visit.

He cried, or at least thought he had. There wasn't much pain, the morphine saw to that but he still hurt. He kind of always knew that this was how things would go but he was scared nonetheless. Not for himself, but for his family. He wanted them to be all right after whatever happened. He wanted them to have safe and happy lives after he was gone. Above all, he wanted his wife to visit. Just to be able to hear her voice just one last time.

He waited. It was all he could do now. Wait for the end, and hope that his wife came by.

Shadow

Meg Dunley

How do you grieve someone still here?

Last year a shadow moved into my son's room, into his soul, and stole him from us. When we admit him into the hospital the shadow of anorexia stares back through his eyes. We cling to tiny, golden moments, few and far between, and gather them like precious gems.

They send us home with our son and Ani—we've named his shadow—and five words: calm, confident, compassionate, consistent, creative.

We grieve what he misses.

We can't see Ani; she's just a shadow, a thin shadow, like the shadows at the end of the day. She slinks in behind him, in front of him, around him. Ani slinks around the house listening, watching, and concocting devious plans. We tell her we won't negotiate with her.

Be like me, she whispers. Her long fingers and nails twist so he can't move without her permission.

We sit with food in front of us; medicine for him, poison for Ani.

Ani whispers into his ear, *Don't trust them, they're trying to kill you.*

Calm, confident, compassionate, consistent, creative.

Winter brings new possibilities. The icy air sucks away the calories.

Window open, window shut. Open. Shut.

Piss off. It's not him, it's her. *Get out of my room you stupid fucking bitch.*

Calm, confident, compassionate, consistent, creative.

Shivering, jiggling. Food in pockets, under seats. Spitting. Nails long to dissect food. It's all inedible.

Come close. She tangles her arms around him. *Let's go for a run.*

I love you, more than they do. She purrs, seduces him. *Trust me.* She strangles him until he can barely breathe. When he gasps she says, *Do you love me?* And he nods in terror. Only then does she let go.

Then do what I want, for me, she purrs.

He jiggles and runs, paces and seals his mouth so no words betray his fear, his terror, his pain. This lover who found him and stole him, has him hostage.

You don't need any other, she says. Don't let them touch you, you've got *me, only me, I'm the only one who loves you enough. We're a team,* she says. She points to his certificates, awards, accolades. We did this together, she says. Not them.

We interrupt her; she writhes and punishes him. She knows we will steal him back one day when she isn't watching, keeping vigil all day and night. His eyes flicker; sleep is coming.

Wake up, she says. *We're not done. Sleep is for the weak. Us? We are strong, disciplined. We can do this. Drink water, just water. Let it cleanse you so you can be pure like me, be rid of all the fat and the bloat. Be strong and pure. Pure discipline. Only the strong can do this. People like you.*

I touch his face, his bony back as he sleeps and whisper, 'I love you.'

Calm, confident, compassionate, consistent, creative.

When The Rain Comes

Lillian Reilly

When you were my mother-in-law I saw you as a hard, loveless woman. Compacted like dry soil by a spirit as mean as the drought that had ruined our land. When I left your son, and the farm, you told me you'd always hated me. That neither you nor your son would ever have contact with me or our baby again.

I tried to tell you that I didn't leave him because I didn't still love him. Or because of the lack of money or the drought or even because he didn't have the courage to climb out from under your smothering wing. I left him because he didn't know how to love me or his son. He had the drought inside him too. A barren place where nothing could grow.

I wanted my son to grow into a man like the men in my family. Funny, warm expansive men who weathered life with passion and courage. So I took my boy back to my family and although I tried, he never saw you or his father again.

You told me of his father's death so cruelly in that brief letter.

'Johnny's dead. Just like his father. Blew his brains out in the hay shed. Happened a fortnight ago but had to have an autopsy. Funeral's on Friday. You can stay at the farm. I live in town now. Hope you appreciate that I'm telling you.'

Now I see you crumpled beside his coffin. Your fingers are trying to find a handhold on the smooth wood. You are keening. A terrible soft wailing that for millennia has floated through air, crossed rivers, echoed over hills and burrowed into the heart of the earth. It is the sound of a mother, her soul naked to the world, grieving her dead child.

I go to you and kneel beside you and you meld into my arms. Lost to grief you have no barriers. I rock and cry with you for the man that was John.

'My son . . .' you cry suddenly.

The anguish in your words makes me tremble. They scrape out of your mouth as if your tongue has to push them into the world. You are inconsolable. Even the Minister is helpless to calm you and begin the service. The small group of mourners sits in edgy embarrassment. Then my son, all fourteen years of him, is beside us. He kneels and wraps you in his arms.

'It's all right, Nanna. I'm here. We'll be right.'

He pulls me close as well. I look at him. His face is tear-streaked. He leads us, tight in his embrace, to the front pew. He sits you between us and when you reach for my hand I know it's true. We will be all right. I catch his eye and his gaze is steadfast and tender. My heart pumps with so much love I can barely contain it. My son.

Visitants

Richard James Allen

They come to me in the night,
as real as people. Perhaps
they are thinking they are the ones
keeping me company, since I too,
like them, seem unable
to be with the sleeping ones.
They are as awake to me
as any persons I have ever met,
even if they are somehow
incomplete, which may be
how I appear to them.
In each other's company we sit
sometimes for eternities,
sometimes moments,
though from this sitting
I now understand
there is no difference.
Nothing is said. Just the resting
of one head against another,
a palm in a hand.
We huddle together,
perched in the dark imagining,
grey-eyed creatures
staring out across
the vast expanse
we have yet to fly,
in this life or those ahead,
unable to divine what elixir
will enlighten our lift off
into the endless firmament,
what wonder will animate
the undulation of our wings,
what grace will soften
our eventual fall into a landing
we can call an arrival.

Grief

Laura Shore

A full-bodied NO
flutes
through the hollows
of my bones, oboes
the sob of my blood.
This one-sided argument
pummels my days.
Even my fingernails crack
at the shock of it.

Our symphony flattens and thins.
Nights swirl empty
of stars.
Dust slams my windows,
seeps under my doors.
My mouth is a desert.
Grit coats my teeth.
My ears throb
with listening.

Your silence,
my uproar.

The Incident

Audrey Molloy

After Jacques Prévert

The dress that she ironed
The heels that she buckled
The kiss thrown from the balcony
The taxi she caught
The wrist that was stamped
The colleagues who greeted her
The drink that someone brought her
The fog that descended
The lift that was offered
The door that she opened
The heels that she stumbled on
The dress that was torn
The weight of his body
The boyfriend who arrived home
The door that was slammed
The bar that he drank in
The streets that he trudged
The shame that burnt in her
The job she couldn't return to
The country they left
The knee he went down on
The answer she gave

Splendour Rock

Chloë Callistemon

we flew a phoenix from his ash
made of dawn and petals and powder
bagpipes piped the sun up and we rose and flung his flash

Jock stood the stone and blew the morning louder
we gathered on the cliffside, hurled handfuls to the east
made of dawn and petals and powder

we'd walked our pilgrimage the day before, each step a breath released
the night spent by fire, under stars, in crackled silence
we gathered on the cliffside, hurled handfuls to the east

where the stained-glass tops of eucalypts flamed in raw tints
our skin lost the grey of the day before
the night spent by fire, under stars, in crackled silence

the sun rose, the wind turned, the crows began to caw
a dirge for other people in other places
our skin lost the grey of the day before

we kindled smiles and tripped into embraces
we flew a phoenix from his ash
laughed as grit blew back into our mouths, eyes, dusted our faces
as bagpipes piped the sun up and we rose and flung his flash

Tilt

Melanie Whybrow

Simon replaced the telephone receiver and returned to the kitchen. He was once again struck by the pretty effect of dappled afternoon light as it shone through the lead glass at the top of the doorway and onto the tiles. It was the feature of this house that most beguiled them when they moved here a quarter of a century ago. But today, it seemed to mock him. The kitchen was quiet and Marg sat unmoving at the table; an untouched mug of cooling tea in front of her.

'We can't have the helmet back,' he said. His wife stirred and looked up at him, as if she was trying to remember who he was, he thought.

'Why not?'

Simon did not know what to say. He sat down opposite her at the table. He felt defeated and unable to continue. Marg was staring at him, her face completely white except for her eyes which were puffy and red-rimmed. He thought she looked shrunken somehow, collapsed in on herself, this woman he had known and loved all his adult life.

'Why can't we have his helmet back?' Marg repeated. Simon looked away, to behind her shoulder to the jumbled assortment of mess on the kitchen sideboard. And there was Toby, smiling out of a snapshot in a small cheap frame. He was standing in his full black and red leathers, beside his beloved bike, his helmet resting on his hip. He beamed at his father from the photo. Like the king of the world, Marg had said that day.

Simon was aware of the sound of his own breathing in the quiet kitchen. He consciously shut his eyes and refocused on his wife. He wanted to reach out a hand to her but the kitchen around him was starting to tilt.

Swallowing hard he tried to organise the police officer's words, exactly.

'The helmet had to be destroyed for safety reasons. It had biological matter inside it,' he said.

'His . . . ' Marg said quietly. 'My son . . . part of my son's brain?' It was almost a whisper.

'I'm sorry, love . . . ' Simon began but Marg rose and left the kitchen.

Simon felt a rushing in his ears and an almost physical sense of free-fall. He put the palms of both hands on the table to steady himself, and breathed. He pushed himself up and snatched the mug, spilling tea. At the sink he stopped and stared down into the bright stainless steel. His thoughts swirled like the indistinct reflections on its surface. He lifted his head and looked out through the kitchen window. He saw his wife in the garden with her back to him. Her shoulders trembled under the thin material of her cardigan. He left the mug in the sink and went out to her.

www.ingramcontent.com/pod-product-compliance
Lightning Source LLC
Chambersburg PA
CBHW060336030426
42336CB00011B/1372